Frantic Frogs
and Other
Frankly Fractured
Folktales for
Readers Theatre

Mrs. Pluto

Frantic Frogs
and Other
Frankly Fractured
Folktales for
Readers Theatre

ANTHONY D. FREDERICKS

Illustrated by
Anthony Allan Stoner
and
Joan Garner

1993
TEACHER IDEAS PRESS
A Division of
Libraries Unlimited, Inc.
Englewood, Colorado

To all my friends with slimy green skin,
big bulging eyes, and an insatiable appetite
for winged insects. (You know who you are!)

TEACHER IDEAS PRESS
A Division of Libraries Unlimited, Inc.
P.O. Box 6633
Englewood, CO 80155-6633
1-800-237-6124

Library of Congress Cataloging-in-Publication Data

Fredericks, Anthony D.
  Frantic frogs and other frankly fractured folktales for readers
theatre / by Anthony D. Fredericks.
    xiii, 123 p. 22x28 cm.
    Includes bibliographical references.
    ISBN 1-56308-174-1
    1. Readers' theater. 2. Fairy tales--Parodies, imitations, etc.
  I. Title.
PN2081.R4F74   1993
808.5'45--dc20   93-25327
                                              CIP

Contents

Part I
READERS THEATRE BEFORE FROGS

Part II
ALL THE REALLY WEIRD AND WACKY STORIES
YOU BOUGHT THIS BOOK FOR

Part III
HOP ON OVER – HERE'S A BUNCH
OF FROG STORIES

Part IV
SOME SHORT STORIES

Part V
APPENDIXES

Acknowledgments

The creation of this book was inspired, encouraged, and supported by many individuals.

A special note of appreciation is extended to Kermit, who has single-handedly elevated amphibians to their rightful place in the animal kingdom. He is an inspiration to all who follow in his footsteps.

To Snow White and Prince Charming, who let me stay at the castle while I was conducting my research down at the swamp, thanks a million! And to the third little pig, who gave me a place to stay during my travels through the enchanted forest—you were terrific! Sorry about your brothers.

A certificate of recognition certainly goes to all the trolls, witches, giants, evil stepmothers, wizards, and other really ugly, bad-tempered, and mean-spirited characters who never seem to get the literary credit they deserve. This one's for you!

My undying gratitude goes to Suzanne Barchers—a princess among editors!

Naturally, my sincerest appreciation goes to that wonderful little frog who allowed me to look inside his guts in biology class at the Orme School in the spring of 1963—he has continued to be an inspiration and will always be remembered for his sacrifice.

A special tip of the hat goes to those wild and crazy three bears down at the lodge. Hugs and kisses for that fantastic going away party. And, wow! Was that terrific porridge, or what?

Of course, no acknowledgment section would be complete without recognizing the devotion, dedication, and longevity of our all-time favorite storyteller—Ma Goose. She has been, and continues to be, an inspiration to children and childlike people everywhere. Without her, this book would not have been possible. Thanks, Mom!

A Bunch of Superfluous Words I
Found Lying Around My Desk
(a.k.a. the Preface)

Stand up in a crowded theater and yell, "AMPHIBIANS!" and what's the first thing people do? They think of frogs, naturally (although, of course, you're always going to get those two or three nut cases who will initially consider toads, but we're not going to even talk about them). Indeed, for some inexplicable reason (translation: the *National Enquirer* hasn't printed the story yet) most people have an affinity for, and an appreciation of, frogs. It's not that most of us have a basement hopping with frogs, it's just that a frog is so, wel-l-l-l-l-l-l-l-l cuddly and cute—in an amphibious sort of way.

Although we, as grown-ups, respect and admire frogs for who they are and what they do, such is not always the case with the younger generation ... which is sort of a roundabout way of telling you about an incident from my early years. You see, way back, a long, long time ago, I was in the fourth grade. My best friend, Bill Callender, and I were inseparable, except for this one time when we got into a humongous argument about who was the best player at dodgeball (we earnestly believed that a single game of dodgeball was the definitive separator of the men from the boys—in fourth-grade terms, that is). In the midst of this loud and raucous argument, my (usually) best friend turned to me and said (with style and panache), "Eat flies, Frog Lips!" I can't remember my actual response to that eloquent put-down; although it was probably something along the lines of "Oh yeah, well your mother wears combat boots" (a falsehood, because in all the times I had dinner at the Callenders' house not once had I ever seen Mrs. C. in anything else but heels or those strange little tennis shoes she always used to wear).

Now to be perfectly honest, up until that point in my childhood I'd never given much thought to the shape and size of my lips (not that lips are an anatomical feature that consumes the thoughts of your average fourth grader). By the same token, I'd never really given much thought to frogs either (please keep in mind that these were the "Good Old Days"—the time before "Sesame Street" and Kermit the Frog). Oh sure, my parents had read me all the usual stories about princes who had been turned into enchanted frogs, each of whom then waited around some poorly drained swampland for a desperate (and "drop dead gorgeous") maiden to come mucking by and plant a big kiss on their slimy lips and transform them back into some macho hunk so that they could live happily ever after, etc., etc., etc.

Nevertheless, a fourth grader's psyche is fragile, and I thought I had been called the worst of the worst. My ego collapsed, I got warts on my hands, and I could no longer wear my favorite green sweater. I felt lower than a snake's belly (another creature that's certainly gotten a lot of bad press in children's literature over the years).

To be perfectly honest, other than a few fairy tales (and one or two late night horror movies) I'd never really had a close association with (or affinity for) frogs.

> **frog** \\'fròg, 'fräg\\ *n., v.,* **frogged, frogging.** *-n* **1.** any of various tailless amphibians (order *Salientia*), esp. of the web-footed aquatic species constituting the genus *Rana* and allied genera.

Despite this gap in my schema (excuse me, that should read "background knowledge"), my teachers were eventually able to provide me with sufficient opportunities to experience and learn about frogs (isn't education great?) throughout the remainder of my schooling. I learned that were it not for frogs, we'd probably be up to our armpits in flies (not that anyone would want to stand around an area that deep in *Musca Domestica*). And, thanks to authors like Mark Twain, I learned that frogs have achieved their rightful place in some of this country's greatest literature. I also discovered:

- The two-inch-long Coqui Frog has a croak that can reach 108 decibels—which is louder than a low-flying jet ("out of the mouths of babes")

- Among frogs, the female is usually larger than the male (does the name "Big Mama" mean anything?)

- Frogs have teeth; toads don't (they just gum their food)

- Bullfrogs croak with their mouths closed (show-offs!)

- Frogs don't drink water; they absorb it through their skin (which is why you never see them in singles bars)

- A frog can't swallow without closing its eyes ("Keep your eyes closed when you chew your food, son.")

- The Goliath Frog of West Africa often reaches a length of more than two and one-half feet (the other frogs in the swamp just call him "Sir").

Indeed, the more I learned about frogs, the more I realized how they, alone, may have had more impact on modern society than any other amphibian (again, we won't even mention those *toads*!). With my newly found knowledge, I found myself disdaining frog legs as a dinner entrée for fear of upsetting the precious ecological balance of some wildlife preserve deep in the Minnesota woods. I began to develop a healthy respect for those frogs who so bravely give their lives so that legions of high school sophomores can dissect and discover the physiological wonders (i.e., the guts) of higher forms of life. In short, I came to realize that the moniker "Frog Lips" may, now, have been more a badge of honor than my friend Bill had originally intended.

Fortunately, I survived that egregious incident of my youth. Along with all my other discoveries about frogs, I came to the realization that frogs may have gotten "the short end of the stick" literature-wise. Oh sure, there are those previously mentioned frogs who hop through a couple of enchanted tales getting kissed by busloads of comely maidens. Yet, for the majority of frogs, that's only a dream. For most frogs, their day-to-day existence is rarely chronicled in anything but fairy tales. They lead a simple life—paddling around some dismal puddle eating truckfuls of winged insects and mating with other frogs so that they can produce thousands and thousands of tadpoles for the armies of schoolchildren to scoop up (during the requisite spring field trip) and take back to thousands of classroom aquariums.

So I began thinking. Why not write a book about frogs (and other storybook characters) who always do traditional things in traditional ways in very traditional stories? For example, don't you think stepmothers, fire-breathing dragons, and that strange couple who lives in the heart of the deep and dark forest need some new plots and story lines? In fact, I thought to myself, Wouldn't it be interesting to turn a few of those old familiar tales upside down and tell them from a completely different point of view? Yes, I said to myself, again. (It is indeed a strange peccadillo of writers that they do a lot of talking with themselves.)

Actually, this whole weird idea wasn't mine—it rightfully belongs to my editor, Suzanne Barchers. Now, if you bought this book at a state reading conference or International Reading Association convention, there's a good chance Suzanne sold it to you. (Do you remember? She was the one with the winsome smile and the funny little green fanny pack strapped to her waist [she is without "frog lips," too].) Anyway, Suzanne is one of those rare editors who recognizes (and, we hope, appreciates) the semi-warped sense of humor of some of her authors (as opposed to the completely warped sense of humor of those authors who write for other publishers). So, one day she called and asked if I would be interested in writing a book of readers theatre scripts using popular fairy tales and the like—but with a decidedly offbeat twist. (By the way, it was Suzanne who came up with the clever title for this book. Notice how she took the consonant blend from the beginning of my last name and wove it into the title. Neat, huh?) Being of sound body but particularly dubious mind, it didn't take me long to agree to this project.

I guess all of this is sort of a bizarre and convoluted way of telling you how this book came to be. Nevertheless, I do hope you find these stories to be successful additions to your reading/ language arts program. I also hope your students discover a few chuckles, chortles, guffaws, and belly laughs within these pages. I know the frogs did. (And by the way, have you ever heard a frog laugh?)

Oh, and since you asked, if you're interested in growing frogs in your classroom you may want to obtain the Critter Condo from Nasco, 901 Janesville Rd., Fort Atkinson, WI 53538, 800-558-9595. Teacher's Pet (catalog no. 56-200-6256) and Grow a Frog (catalog no. 56-110-0296) are available from Delta Education, P.O. Box 950, Hudson, NH 03051, 800-442-5444. An excellent video, *Tadpoles and Frogs* (catalog no. 51218) is available from the National Geographic Society, Washington, DC 20036, 800-368-2728. For an informative book on frogs you'll surely want to get *Amazing Frogs and Toads* by Barry Clarke (New York: Knopf, 1990).

Anthony D. Fredericks (a.k.a. "Frog Lips")

Part I

READERS THEATRE
BEFORE FROGS

SOME IMPORTANT STUFF BEFORE
THE REALLY GOOD STUFF
(a.k.a. the Introduction)

"ONCE UPON A TIME...."

Certainly the four most wondrous words in the English language (or any language, for that matter) must be, "Once upon a time." Those words conjure up all sorts of visions and possibilities — faraway lands, magnificent adventures, enchanted princes, beautiful princesses, evil wizards and wicked witches, a few dragons and demons, a couple of castles and cottages, perhaps a mysterious forest or two, and certainly tales of mystery, intrigue, and adventure. These are stories of tradition and timelessness, tales that enchant, mystify, and excite through a marvelous weaving of characters, settings, and plots — tales that have stood the test of time. These are stories of our youth, stories of our heritage, and stories that continue to enrapture audiences with their delightful blending of good over evil, patience over greed, and right over might. Our senses are stimulated, our mental images are energized, and our experiences are fortified with that most magical preface — "Once upon a time...."

The magic of storytelling has been a tradition of every culture and civilization since the dawn of language. It binds human beings and celebrates their heritage as no other language art can. It is part and parcel of the human experience because it underscores the values and experiences we cherish as well as those we seek to share with each other. Nowhere is this more necessary than in today's classroom. Young children, who have been bombarded with visual messages (i.e., television) since birth, still relish and appreciate the power and majesty of a story well told. Even adults, with their hustle-and-bustle lifestyles, enjoy the magic of a story or the enchantment of a storyteller. Perhaps it is a natural part of who we are that stories command our attention and help us appreciate the values, ideas, and traditions we hold dear. So too, should students have those same experiences and those same pleasures.

WHAT IS READERS THEATRE?

Readers theatre is a storytelling device that stimulates the imagination and promotes *all* of the language arts. Simply stated, it is an oral interpretation of a piece of literature read in a dramatic style. But its value extends far beyond that simple definition. Readers theatre is an act of involvement, an opportunity to share, a time to creatively interact with others, and a personal interpretation of what can be or could be. Here's another definition of readers theatre:

Readers theatre is an interpretive reading activity for all the children in the classroom. Readers bring characters to life through their voices and gestures. Listeners are captivated by the vitalized stories and complete the activity by imagining the details of scene and action.... Used in the classroom, readers theatre becomes an integrated language event centering upon oral interpretation of literature. The children adapt and present the material of their choice. A story, a poem, a scene from a play, even a song lyric, provide the ingredients for the script. As a thinking, reading, writing, speaking and listening experience, readers theatre makes a unique contribution to our language arts curriculum. (Sloyer 1982, 3)

It is evident that readers theatre holds the promise of helping students understand and appreciate the richness of language, the ways in which to interpret that language, and how language can be a powerful vehicle for the comprehension and appreciation of different forms of literature. Readers theatre provides numerous opportunities for youngsters to make stories and literature come alive and pulsate with their own unique brand of interpretation and vision. In so doing, literature becomes personal and reflective, and students have a plethora of opportunities to be authentic users of language.

WHAT IS THE VALUE OF READERS THEATRE?

I like to think of readers theatre as a way to interpret literature without the constraints of skills, memorization, or artificial structures (e.g., lots of props, costumes, and elaborate staging). Readers theatre allows students to breathe life and substance into literature—an interpretation that is neither right nor wrong because it will be colored by students' unique perspectives, experiences, and vision. It is, in fact, the readers' interpretation of a piece of literature or a familiar story that is intrinsically more valuable than some predetermined or preordained translation (something that might be found in a teacher's manual or curriculum guide, for example).

With that in mind, I'd like to share with you some of the many values I see in readers theatre:

- It stimulates curiosity and enthusiasm for different forms of literature. It allows students to experience stories in a supportive and nonthreatening format that underscores their active involvement.

- Because readers theatre allows students many different interpretations of the same story, it facilitates the development of critical and creative thinking. There is no such thing as a right or wrong interpretation of a story ... readers theatre validates that assumption.

- Readers theatre focuses on all of the language arts—reading, writing, speaking, and listening. It supports a whole language philosophy of instruction and allows children to become responsible learners—ones who seek out answers to their own self-initiated inquiries.

- Because it is the performance that drives readers theatre, children are given more opportunities to invest themselves and their personalities in the production. The same story may be subject to several different presentations depending on the group or the individual youngsters involved. As such, students learn that readers theatre (as with other forms of literature) can be explored in a host of ways and a host of possibilities.

- Students are given numerous opportunities to learn about the major features of children's literature—plot, theme, setting, point of view, and characterization—particularly when they are provided with opportunities to design and construct their own readers theatre scripts and are given unlimited opportunities to discover the wide variations that can be derived from a single piece.

- Readers theatre is a participatory event. The characters and the audience are both intimately involved in the design, structure, and delivery of the story. As such, students begin to realize that reading is not a solitary activity but one that can be shared and discussed with others.

- Readers theatre is informal and relaxed. It does not require elaborate props, scenery, or costumes. It can be set up in any classroom or learning environment. It does not require large sums of money to "make it happen." And, it can take place in any kind of classroom environment.

- Readers theatre stimulates the imagination and the creation of visual images. It has been substantiated that when youngsters are provided with opportunities to create their own mental images, their comprehension and appreciation of a piece of writing increases considerably. Because only a modicum of formal props and set up is required for any readers theatre production, the participants and audience are encouraged to create supplemental props in their minds—props that may be more elaborate and exquisite than those found in the most lavish of plays.

- Readers theatre enhances the development of cooperative learning strategies. It requires youngsters to work together toward a common goal and supports their efforts in doing so. Readers theatre is not a competitive activity, but rather a cooperative one in which students share, discuss, and band together for the good of the production.

- Readers theatre is valuable for non-English speaking students or nonfluent readers. It provides them with positive models of language usage and interpretation that extend far beyond the decoding of printed materials. It allows them to see language in action and the various ways in which language can be used.

- Teachers have also discovered that readers theatre is an excellent way in which to enhance the development of communication skills. Voice projection, intonation, inflection, and pronunciation skills are all promoted within and throughout any readers theatre production. Students who need assistance in these areas are provided with a support structure that encourages the development of necessary abilities.

- The development and enhancement of self-concept is facilitated through readers theatre. Because children are working in concert with other students in a supportive atmosphere, their self-esteem mushrooms accordingly. Again, the emphasis is on the presentation, not necessarily the performers. As such, youngsters have opportunities to develop levels of self-confidence and self-assurance that would not normally be available in more traditional class productions.

- Creative and critical thinking are enhanced through the utilization of readers theatre. Students are active participants in the interpretation and delivery of a story; as such, they develop thinking skills that are divergent rather than convergent, and interpretive skills that are supported rather than directed.

- When students are provided with opportunities to write or script their own readers theatre, their writing abilities are supported and encouraged. As students become familiar with the design and format of readers theatre scripts, they can begin to utilize their own creative talents in designing their own scripts and stories.

- Readers theatre is fun. Students of all ages have delighted in using readers theatre for many years. It is stimulating and enjoyable, encouraging and fascinating, relevant and personal. Indeed, try as I might, I have not been able to locate a single instance (or group of students) in which (or for whom) readers theatre would not be an appropriate language arts activity. It is a strategy filled with a cornucopia of possibilities and promises.

HOW TO PRESENT READERS THEATRE

It is important to remember that there is no single way to present readers theatre. What I will share with you here are some considerations you and your students may wish to keep in mind as you put on any of the productions in this book. Different classes and even different groups of students within the same class will each have their own method and mode of presentation—in other words, no two presentations may ever be the same. That is certainly one of the best attributes of readers theatre. However, you may wish to consider some of the following when producing and presenting the scripts in this book or scripts created by your students:

- Much of the setting for a story should take place in the audience's mind. Elaborate scenes or scenery are not necessary. A branch or potted plant can serve as a tree; a paper cutout can serve as a tie, badge, or some other attachment; and a hand-lettered sign can be used to designate one part of the staging area as a particular scene (e.g., swamp, castle, field, forest).

- Usually all of the characters will be on stage throughout the duration of the presentation. It is not necessary to have characters enter and exit the presentation. If you place the characters on stools, they can face the audience when they are involved in a particular scene and then turn around whenever they are not involved in a scene. You may wish to make simple hand-lettered signs with the names of each character. Loop a piece of string or yarn through each sign and hang it around the neck of the respective character. The audience then will know the identity of each character throughout the presentation.

- Most presentations will have a narrator to set up the story. The narrator establishes the place and time of the story for the audience so that the characters can "jump into" their parts from the beginning of the story. Typically, the narrator is separated from the other actors and can be identified by a simple sign.

- Several copies of the script should be duplicated (one for each actor). Each set can be bound between two sheets of colored construction paper or poster board. This tends to formalize the presentation a little and lends an air of professionalism to the actors. You may wish to highlight each character's speaking parts with a yellow or pink highlighter pen.

- The readers should have an opportunity to practice their script before presenting it to an audience. Take some time to discuss voice intonation, facial gestures, body movements, and other features that could be used to enhance the presentation. Be encouraging by allowing students the opportunity to suggest their own modifications, adaptations, or interpretations of the script. They will undoubtedly be in tune with the interests and perceptions of their peers, thereby offering some distinctive and personal interpretations.

- The characters should focus on the audience rather than on each other. Practicing the script beforehand can eliminate this problem and help students understand the need to involve the audience as much as possible in the development of the story. Here, voice projection and delivery are important to enable the audience to understand character actions. The proper mood and intent need to be established—and can be when students are familiar and comfortable with each character's style.

- Students should not memorize their lines, but should instead rehearse them sufficiently so that they are comfortable with them. Again, the emphasis is on delivery, so be sure to suggest different tones of voice (e.g., angry, irritated, calm, frustrated, excited) for students to use for their particular character(s).

Presenting a readers theatre script need not be an elaborate or extensive production. As students become more familiar and polished in using readers theatre, they will be able to suggest a multitude of presentation possibilities for future scripts. It is important to help students assume a measure of self-initiated responsibility in the delivery of any readers theatre. In so doing, you will be helping to ensure their personal engagement and active participation in this most valuable of language arts activities.

HOW TO CREATE YOUR OWN
READERS THEATRE

It is hoped that you and your students will find an abundance of readers theatre scripts in this book for use in your classroom. But these scripts should also serve as an impetus for the creation of your own classroom scripts. By providing opportunities for your students to begin designing their own readers theatre scripts, you will be offering them an exciting new arena for the utilization and enhancement of their writing abilities.

Following are some suggestions you and your students may wish to consider in developing readers theatre scripts. They are purposely generic in nature and can be used with almost all kinds of reading material. Of course, the emphasis in this book is on humorous readers theatre scripts— particularly those dealing with fairy tales, Mother Goose rhymes, fables, legends, and other children's classics; thus, these ideas will help your students create their own fractured fairy tales as part of their process writing program.

Select an Appropriate Story

Humor works best when it touches something with which we are familiar. For this reason, the stories selected for this book have come from the experiential background of most students— legends, tall tales, fairy tales and the like—and then have been expanded far beyond their original design. The stories students select for the development of their own readers theatre scripts should also be familiar ones. In so doing, they will be able to build upon that familiarity for a humorous effect.

Appendix A is a bibliography of fairy tales, books, and stories that will provide you with some possibilities and ideas for use in the creation of original readers theatre scripts. These examples represent a wide range of stories from many different lands and many different times. An attempt has been made to include tales that are very familiar to youngsters, as well as others that students will also enjoy. All of the listed stories and tales have been selected for their dramatic appeal and their adaptability to a readers theatre script. I have found, however, that most, if not all, fairy tales and Mother Goose rhymes can be adapted to a readers theatre format ... it just depends on how warped one's sense of humor is. Nevertheless, the best kind of stories to use are those with tight plots and clear endings, distinctive characters, engaging dialogue, and universal themes (e.g., good over evil, love conquers all, logic is more powerful than strength).

In selecting stories, the number of characters needs to be considered as well. I have found that two to six characters work best. For that reason, some minor characters may be eliminated and their dialogue absorbed by other characters; on the other hand, one or two brand new characters may need to be developed to facilitate the pace of the story. It is important that the staging area is not crowded with too many characters, thus hindering the audience's attention.

Illustrate and Model

Initially, students may be unfamiliar with the format of readers theatre (although, after experiencing several of the scripts in this book they will be quite used to the design). Discuss with students that readers theatre scripts are very similar to movie and television scripts and are written in much the same way. As in Hollywood, the intent is to take a basic story and turn it into a play or movie. With your students, discuss the original stories used as the foundation of these scripts and the resultant readers theatre design(s).

Lead your class in a whole group activity to model the steps used in designing a readers theatre script. I have found it advantageous to use a sheet of chart pack paper, a large piece of poster board, or the overhead projector. Using a familiar story, I begin to rewrite it so that the entire class can see the steps I use. These steps might include:

- Rewriting the title to give it a more humorous slant

- Eliminating unnecessary dialogue or minor characters

- Inserting a narrator at strategic points to advance the action or identify specific scenes

- Adding words that describe the tone of voice used by a specific character (e.g., rapidly, irritated, confused)

- Underlining or bold-facing the names of characters for easy identification

- Creating new dialogue, characters, or settings to advance the story or produce a humorous situation

- Considering the props necessary for the story

It should be pointed out that there is no ideal series of steps to follow in the design of readers theatre scripts. It is important, however, that students have some models to follow so that they will be encouraged and supported in the creation of their own scripts.

Adapting the Story

After students have experienced the scripts in this book they will become familiar with ways in which a familiar famous fairy tale or legend can be turned into a humorous readers theatre script. When you allow your students opportunities to develop their own humorous scripts, you will soon discover a wonderfully creative spirit permeating all aspects of your language arts program.

Obviously, humor comes in many forms. Here are some methods you and your students may wish to consider in transforming familiar tales into wild and wacky ones:

Exaggeration. Blow something completely out of proportion. Instead of "Beauty and the Beast," title a revised version "Beauty and This Incredibly Ugly Guy." In place of "Humpty Dumpty" use "This Very Round Fellow Who Sits on Top of a Wall All Day Long." Exaggeration can extend beyond story titles to character personalities and physical descriptions as well as story settings.

Colloquialisms. Allow students to use language and idioms with which they are most familiar (some mild censorship may be necessary). Slang terms and phrases from the mouths of familiar characters can be quite funny. For example, Little Red Riding Hood could say to the wolf, "Look, dude, mess around with me and you'll be eating a knuckle sandwich for dinner." Or Snow White could say to the evil stepmother, "Hey, stop buggin' me. I've had it up to here with your stupid poison apples." Obviously, a selective use of colloquialisms is preferable to a script rife with slang.

Reversals. Change characters' personalities so that they are completely different. For example, instead of the typical evil stepmother, have students create a really nice stepmother; instead of an enchanted prince, have students develop a fairly stupid prince; instead of a fire-breathing dragon, have students create a shy reptile trying to kick the smoking habit. Reversals (or partial reversals) can be used for the setting of a story, too. Instead of a gingerbread house, have students design a condo in the suburbs; instead of a stinky swamp, have students use a beach in Hawaii; and instead of a deep, dark forest, have students set a story in a shopping mall.

Anachronisms. Use an object that is totally out of place in the story. For example, instead of having the wicked witch travel on a broomstick, she can use her frequent flyer miles on an airplane; instead of characters traveling from one castle to another, they can call each other on their cellular phones; instead of sending a poison pen letter by messenger, it can be faxed.

Misdirection. Misdirection takes place when the reader or listener is misled as to the outcome of a story. For example, the story of Hansel and Gretel can be told as originally written except with a new ending in which the witch is eaten by the children. For another story, Cinderella could go to the ball and meet the handsome prince, but then go home and get sick on pumpkin pie.

Character changes. Give familiar characters entirely new personalities or whole new physical features. For example, the wicked wizard could finally get a full-time job and give up his part-time incantations. The fire-breathing dragon could get a loan from the bank and market his own brand of barbecue sauce. The enchanted prince could develop a bad case of halitosis and be unable to get anyone to kiss him. The troll could go to charm school and learn to eat with a knife and fork.

Combination formula. Using a combination formula, the writer combines two very different subjects or elements into an entirely new arrangement. For example, the eating habits of a frog can be combined with the eating habits of a prince to create a prince who sits around the castle all day snatching flies out of the air with his three-foot tongue. The personality of a frog can be combined with the personality of a real estate developer to create an amphibian who sells swampland in Florida. The features of a fairy tale cottage can be combined with the features of a suburban housing development to create a development of condos for wicked witches only (no young children allowed).

Preparation and Writing

Students should be encouraged to work together to design their readers theatre scripts. Small groups of four to five students will allow for a multiplicity of options and suggestions for scripting a familiar story. It would be advantageous to appoint one student within each group to serve as the *scribe* or *recorder*. Each recorder should understand that writing goes through many stages and that the first couple of story plots are just that—initial ideas that can be eliminated or expanded according to the wishes and desires of the group.

Have each group's recorder write the names of all of the identified characters down the left side of a large sheet of poster paper. Other members of a group can suggest possible dialogue for each of the characters as well as the narrator. Movements and actions can also be suggested by group members. I have found it advantageous to consider any props, stage directions, and set up *after* the initial draft of the script. In this way, students can concentrate on the creative expression of their ideas without worrying about some of the minor aspects of their script—all of which can be added later.

Production and Practice

Provide student groups with opportunities to try out their drafts on other groups of students. They should monitor the flow of the story, the pace, appropriate dialogue, and, of course, the humor of their script. Just as a playwright will go through many drafts of a play, so too should your students realize that they may also need time to work out the kinks in their productions. By trying out their various drafts on other students, they will have an opportunity to structure and restructure their readers theatre script for maximum impact.

YES, WE EVEN HAVE A SECTION ON EVALUATION!

To be effective, evaluation must be a continuous process. It must also engage students in the design of their own learning objectives and provide both teachers and students with useful data that can be employed to enhance learning opportunities. In that light, evaluation is much, much more than the traditional pen-and-paper tests of yesterday; rather, it is more a process of reaction, reflection, and redirection. It is certainly much more than the simple administration of a test and the recording of resultant scores. It is a combination of factors and forces that should have a positive impact on children's literacy growth and development.

Any effective evaluation program

- is continuous and ongoing—a constant process of evolution;

- emphasizes a variety of evaluative tools and devices in line with students' different needs, abilities, and interests;

- promotes a collaborative spirit between and among students and teachers—it is not something *done to* students, but rather something *done with* students; and

- needs to be authentic in nature—reflective of students' developing literacy skills and supportive of their self-initiated ventures into the world of books and literature.

I'm certainly not suggesting that you need to initiate a new form of evaluation solely for the readers theatre scripts you use in your classroom. Nor do I mean to imply that readers theatre even needs to be evaluated with some of the more traditional methods. Readers theatre, in and of itself, should be a pleasurable and stimulating experience for students. Attaching an evaluation component to each and every readers theatre script may rob children of the excitement and spontaneity that so often permeates this language arts activity.

However, if you are interested in using readers theatre as a regular part of your language arts program, you may wish to consider some of the following as appropriate for your entire evaluation process. This list is certainly not meant to be finite or complete. It's important that you also talk with your students about other evaluative measures that support the four guidelines suggested above.

1. After a presentation, have all members of the class engage in a discussion about the impact of the story. What could be done to improve it? Why? Any suggested changes or modifications?

2. Use anecdotal records to record the participation of members of the cast as well as members of the audience. Were they engaged? Were they excited? Were they actively involved?

3. Provide several members of the audience with feedback forms in which they respond to such elements as expression, involvement, presentation, and excitement or other aspects of a selected performance.

4. Identify three or four students in the audience to mark a checklist which has been designed by the whole class. The checklist can be turned over to cast members who can use it as a part of their own evaluation of the performance.

5. Simple observational records by individuals from other classes can be developed and completed.

6. Photographs or a video can be taken of a specific presentation and analyzed later by cast members or the whole class.

7. Self-assessment forms can be developed by each production team. These can be discussed by the cast after a presentation and their findings shared with the entire class.

8. A project log (including the drafting, preparation, and presentation) of a readers theatre script can be maintained by a group of students. The log can become part of a larger classroom portfolio or turned over to the teacher for comments and discussion.

9. All student members of a production crew can maintain a reading response log which records their thoughts and perceptions about the development and presentation of a specific readers theatre script.

Evaluation should offer students opportunities for growth and improvement. As stated above, however, it is certainly not necessary or essential to evaluate everything your students do in readers theatre. It is important that you are sensitive to the interest factor involved with readers theatre and that you not diminish it with constant assessment and evaluation. Also, be aware that evaluation affects students' developing self-concepts as much as their developing academic skills. *How* you evaluate is just as important as *what* you evaluate.

REFERENCES

Sloyer, Shirley. *Readers Theatre: Story Dramatization in the Classroom*. Urbana, IL: National Council of Teachers of English, 1982.

Part II
ALL THE REALLY WEIRD
AND WACKY STORIES
YOU BOUGHT THIS BOOK FOR

ONCE UPON A....

STAGING:

The narrator and the two characters can be standing or seated on stools. They should address each other rather than the audience.

	Frog #1	*Frog #2*
	X	X

Narrator
X

NARRATOR: Once upon a time in a land far, far away there lived....

FROG #1: Hey, Narrator, don't you think it's about time you came up with something just a little more original than "Once upon a time ..."? I mean, throughout history, every narrator like you has started each story with "Once upon a time...." Now, I don't know about those other guys in all those other stories, but frankly, it's starting to get on my nerves.

NARRATOR: Well, okay, how about this. Long ago, in a far distant kingdom....

FROG #2: Oh, come on, get real. What kid is going to listen to a story that begins like that? Look, these are the '90s—how about something a little spicier, something with meat on it?

NARRATOR: Well, if you two think you're so smart, how about you coming up with some kind of dynamic opening?

FROG #1: Okay. How about this.... Two incredibly handsome and intelligent frogs were sitting on their lily pads when this really gorgeous woman comes waltzing down to the swamp to go swimming.

NARRATOR: *(sarcastically)* You think kids today are going to believe that two frogs like you are so smart when all you do is sit around a swamp eating flies all day long? And what are you going to do with this incredibly raving beauty—have her kiss you all over the face? Yeah, right. Like some model in a swimsuit is going to dash down to her local swamp and kiss the first slimy creature she meets. Either she's desperate or about as dumb as a flagpole.

FROG #1: *(defiantly)* Hey, listen here, Mr. Smarty-pants Narrator. You challenged us to create a better story beginning for this tale than you did, and I think we've done all right. It's certainly a lot more interesting than that "Once upon a time ..." mish-mash that YOU use.

FROG #2: Yeah, so there!

NARRATOR: You must think kids are really stupid if they're going to take the word of two frogs who do nothing more than slop around in yucky mud all day and suck on grass-hoppers for dinner every night.

FROG #1: *(argumentatively)* Look, all we're trying to do is get kids interested in our life story. After all, we're two of the coolest dudes from Swampville, U.S.A. We just want the whole world to know it, too.

NARRATOR: Hey, get a life! These are fairy tales—stories created to stimulate the imagination and get children interested in reading more about the world around them.

FROG #2: *(sarcastically)* Yeah, like they're going to flip off MTV just to listen to some dodo in a coat and tie tell them about some talking animals and beautiful princesses who run around all day kissing every green creature they see.

NARRATOR: Hey, listen. These stories have been handed down for centuries. They have survived wars, changes in governments, and will last far longer than any rock video you can name. Besides, they're fun.

FROG #1: Well, maybe so. But just don't forget about us. We may suck grasshoppers all day, but we've got great personalities. The least you could do is give us some starring roles!

NARRATOR: Okay. I'll see what I can do. In the meantime, why don't you guys grab a couple of flies, I'll bring some bottled swamp water, and we'll cruise on over to the salaman-der's house ... AND LET'S PARTY!!!

LITTLE MISS MUFFET SMASHES THE SPIDER TO SMITHEREENS

STAGING:

The narrator stands at a podium. Miss Muffet should sit in a chair. The other characters should all be standing and should approach Miss Muffet in turn, as they speak.

	Caterpillar	*Turtle*	*Bird*	*Snake*	*Spider*
	X	X	X	X	X

Miss Muffet
X

Narrator
X

NARRATOR: Once upon a time there was this little girl — Miss Muffet by name — who used to sit around all day eating bowls of curds and whey. Frankly, I think she was just a little touched in the head; I mean who in their right mind would even *think* about eating curds and whey? Well, anyway, she would sit around the yard on her tuffet (and if you don't know what a tuffet is, don't ask!) and chow down on all those weird dairy products from the olden days. For some reason, this kind of activity seemed to attract all kinds of creatures and critters from the nearby forest. (You know how there's always a deep, dark forest in all these stories.) Well, anyway, these animals also liked the curds and whey and would sit near Miss Muffet with their tongues hanging out of their mouths, hoping for some handouts or at least a few licks of her bowl. So, let's look in on a recent encounter.

MISS MUFFET: *(insistently)* Hey, look guys, all I want to do is just sit here and eat my curds and whey in peace and quiet. I don't bother you ... you don't bother me. Okay?

CATERPILLAR: *(to the audience)* First of all, you're probably wondering how a caterpillar gets a major role in a story like this. You may even be wondering how a caterpillar winds up with a SPEAKING role. Well, let's just say I've got a great agent who really knows her Mother Goose stories. *(to Miss Muffet)* I'd sure like to get a taste of that stuff in your bowl, Muffet lady. All I get to eat is a bunch of dirty old leaves and a couple of blades of grass. Some curds and whey would be great right about now.

MISS MUFFET: *(angrily)* Bug off! Just let me eat my dinner by myself.

TURTLE: Boy, are we getting grouchy, or what? You think you've got it rough. How about me? All I get to eat is some lettuce and handfuls of rotten vegetables. And to top it all off, I have to race some smarty-pants rabbit next week down by the lake. I don't know about you, but I've just about had it! And just to make things worse than they are, how about those teenage cousins of mine who get to spend their lives in the city sewer and eat all the pizza they want. Do you think they'd share some of that with me? N-o-o-o-o-o-o-o-o-o-o!

MISS MUFFET: *(defiantly)* You know, you guys are beginning to get on my nerves. Don't you have something better to do than bother some poor innocent young girl just trying to eat her dinner?

NARRATOR: It seems as though Miss Muffet is beginning to get a little testy. Let's keep listening and see what she does.

BIRD: *(happily)* Hey good lookin', how 'bout sharing some of that stuff with me? You know, it's not easy living on a steady diet of worms and other creepy, crawling things. Wow, talk about your indigestion! A little curds and whey now and again would be just the ticket for my upset stomach.

MISS MUFFET: *(really angrily)* Why don't you all just take a hike! You're really starting to get on my nerves. Can't you simply leave me alone so I can eat my meal in peace?

SNAKE: *(slowly)* S-s-s-s-s-s-s-s-s-s-s-s-say ... mind if I join you? I was just slithering through the area and thought I smelled something delicious. You wouldn't happen to have some extras for a lowlife like me, now would you?

MISS MUFFET: *(very angrily)* That does it! The next guy who comes along and bothers me while I'm eating is going to get it ... and I'm not kidding! You read me?

SPIDER: Excuse me, I was just wond....

NARRATOR: *(loudly and forcefully)* WHAM! WHAM! WHAM! SQUISH! SQUISH! SQUISH! WHAM! WHAM! WHAM! And so it was that Miss Muffet smashed that poor, little, innocent, defenseless, tiny, shy, timid spider to smithereens. The other animals quickly got the hint and left her alone to eat her curds and whey. And they never bothered her again.

COUGHY, THE DWARF SNOW WHITE
NEVER TOLD YOU ABOUT

STAGING:

The narrator sits on a high stool in the front center of the staging area. The other characters can be standing or sitting on stools.

	Doc	Dopey		Sleepy
	X	X		X
Happy		Grumpy	Sneezy	Bashful
X		X	X	X
	Narrator		Snow White	
	X		X	

NARRATOR: *(sometimes rambling)* Now, you know how these stories go. See, there's this "Once upon a time" part of the story that tells you when and where the story took place. Then there's this little ditty about some wonderfully beautiful princess or some incredible hunk of a prince who meet each other, are separated by some ragged old witch or a wicked wizard with an attitude problem, and then by the end of the story are reunited to live happily ever after. You've heard one, you've heard them all, right? Think about it. Just how many beautiful princesses and handsome princes are there? I mean, look at me … I'm good lookin', handsome, bright, intelligent, and so-o-o-o-o-o incredibly smart, but do you see me putting on some green leotards to go prancing around some deep, dark forest to look for some drop-dead gorgeous princess who wants to be rescued from an evil spell? Come on, let's get real! I've sure got better things to do with my time. But anyway, on with this story, which is about this girl who just happens to find herself in the midst of a deep, dark forest, having been put there by her evil (what else) stepmother. She's obviously lost and alone and frightened and cold and all that other stuff when she just happens to come upon a small cottage in the middle of the woods (how convenient). So she walks in, finds nobody home, and decides to pick up a broom and clean out the place (just like they do in all those other stories). Anyway, she's polishing the silverware and scrubbing the floors when the real occupants of the house come home from work. They're small, tiny, short, undersized, little men. That's right, you guessed it, the seven dwarfs. Except in this story there's another little dwarf who was left out of the original version. Of course there's Dopey, and Sneezy, and Doc, and Sleepy, and Grumpy, and Happy, and Bashful. But this new dwarf … his name is Coughy. Why? Well, duh, it's probably because he coughs a lot. Anyway, on with the story.

19

SNOW WHITE: *(with surprise)* My goodness, look at you all. How did you all get to be so short?

SNEEZY: *(irritated)* Look, lady. Just answer this. How did you get in our house and who invited you here, anyway?

SNOW WHITE: Well, you see, the narrator said it was okay to just walk in here and start the story from this point.

NARRATOR: Hey, don't look at me, guys. I just work here.

DOC: *(defiantly)* Yeah, well, just what makes you think you can just waltz in here any time you like, clean our house, and become an important character in our story? Do you think you're some fancy-pants, young model who can do just anything she wants and get away with it? Well, I've got news for you, sister. This here's the real "Deep, Dark Forest," and we don't allow just any character to crawl into our house any old time she wishes just so she can get a starring role in a story.

DOPEY: *(slowly)* Yeah, just remember what happened to that Goldilocks woman. You heard what she got for that breaking-and-entering episode in the Three Bears' house on the other side of the forest. So, you'd better just watch yourself, sister!

SLEEPY: *(snappily)* So what's your story, White? In fact, I bet your last name isn't even White. I bet it's Ball, or Drift, or Storm, or something like that. White's probably just a made-up name you use in these stories. Isn't that right?

SNOW WHITE: *(defensively)* No, really, it's White, Snow White. You see, I was born one dark morning during the middle of a blinding snowstorm and my father couldn't....

GRUMPY: *(slightly angry)* Look, we've all heard that sad tale before, and believe me, we don't buy it for one second. Who do you think you're foolin'?

DOC: Let's get back to the real issue here. How come you're in our house washing our pots and pans and sweeping our floor? Maybe, just maybe, we happen to like being slobs. Did you ever think about that? What makes you think that just because there's garbage all over our cottage and dust and dirt everywhere that you have a right to come in and clean it up? We happen to like living this way. I mean, look at all the boys and girls out in the audience. Aren't their rooms messy and dirty? Don't they have dirty clothes all over the floor and messy beds? Don't they like to live like slobs, too? You're darn right they do. So, what are you going to do ... visit each and every one of THEIR homes and clean them up? Fat chance!

HAPPY: *(smiling)* Yeah, Doc's right. We just happen to like living like pigs. Is there any law against that?

BASHFUL: *(shyly)* And that certainly doesn't give you any right to come in here in the middle of a nice lovely story and start all this dust flying around.

SNOW WHITE: Hey, guys, ease up! I was just trying to help. Besides, I thought it might be a nice way to get this story moving along. After all, the kids in the audience are pretty familiar with the original story, and I thought this would be a good way to get the new story off the ground. Oh, my gosh. I forgot about the new story. I was supposed to tell them about your cousin, Coughy.

DOC: *(irritated)* Now see what you've gone and done. You've spent so much time on this supposedly great introduction to the story that we're all out of time for the rest of the story. Thanks a lot!!!

NARRATOR: *(at times rambling)* Well, as it were, Snow White was never able to tell the story about the eighth dwarf, Coughy. But just so you don't feel totally left out, Coughy was later sent to the castle, the one where the evil stepmother lived, to pick up a prescription for his cough. He got a coughing attack just as the evil stepmother was walking by the drugstore, and he coughed all over her. The evil stepmother came down with a case of pneumonia and died a short time later. Coughy became a hero to all the townspeople and eventually had a statue erected in the center of town in his honor. Some talent agency signed him to appear in a TV commercial for a new cold medicine. He eventually wound up making a lot of money and retiring to a condo in Hawaii (which is why you never hear about him in the usual Snow White stories). The other dwarfs have to continue working in the diamond mine to try and earn a living. And Snow White ... well, she just keeps going through the forest cleaning up all the cottages she can find.

BEAUTY AND THIS INCREDIBLY UGLY GUY

STAGING:

Narrator I can stand to the left of the staging area; Narrator II can stand to the right. The two characters can sit on high stools or chairs in the center. They may wish to use plastic toy phones as props.

                    Ugly Guy   *Beauty*
                        X   X

Narrator I   *Narrator II*
      X   X

NARRATOR I: *(rambling rapidly)* Once upon a time there was this deep, dark forest in which there was a little cottage where this man and this woman lived with all their children and all the animals of the forest would be their friends and they ate berries and leaves and everyone was happy and smiling and just wanted to be left alone so they could eventually live happily ever after, except these out-of-work storytellers came wandering through the forest one day and decided to turn the family's life into some incredibly neat fairy tale or fable or legend or something like that so they would all become incredibly rich and be able to live happily ever after for the rest of their lives, but do you think they even thought of sharing all their riches with that family deep in the enchanted forest? No, of course they didn't, but that's probably another story, which I don't have time to tell you because I'm trying to tell you this story that really isn't a real story, but just a story I made up because I wanted to get rich and famous like all those other storytellers, so what I did was take one of their stories—actually I just borrowed it for a while—and changed just a couple of the facts and events— well, maybe I changed a lot of the facts and events—so that I could tell it to you and you would become incredibly excited and want to hear it again and again, and want to tell your friends about this story and they would want to hear it again and again, and, of course, I would become very rich and very famous and invite you all over to my castle and give you a ride in my incredibly fast carriage, but maybe I'm getting ahead of myself. Perhaps I'd better just tell you the story and see if you like it first—okay, okay, okay. Well, anyway, here goes!

(more slowly) Once upon a time there was this really gorgeous-looking, blonde maiden, I mean a real knockout, a real beauty, with a fantastic personality and everything. As you might expect, all the princes from the local castle wanted to date her and take her to movies and concerts, and do all the other kinds of things guys do with incredibly beautiful maidens. But this incredibly ravishing young maiden didn't like all the young men in the castle, most of whom were about as stupid as a doormat anyway. Well, it just so happened that there was this really, ugly guy over in the next castle. I mean, you talk about ugly ... he was so bad he made paint peel just by being in a room. He was so ugly he had to put a bag over his head just to sneak up on a glass of water to take a drink. He was so ugly that dogs would howl whenever he walked by. He was so ugly....

NARRATOR II: Will you just get on with the story, already?

NARRATOR I: Okay, okay. So anyway, this really, really, really, ugly guy wants to take this fantastically stunning young maiden out for a date. So he calls her up one evening.

UGLY GUY: Good evening, may I please speak to the phenomenally stunning young maiden, please. *(pause)* Thank you.

Hello, wonderfully gorgeous young maiden. This is the incredibly ugly guy.

BEAUTY: Oh, hello. Don't you sit behind me in math class?

UGLY GUY: Yeah, that's me. I thought you never noticed me.

BEAUTY: Well, actually, I haven't. It's just that all the other girls have been talkin' about you. So what do you want?

UGLY GUY: *(shyly)* Wel-l-l-l-l-l-l-l-l. You see. The Fall Ball is coming up in a few weeks down at the castle. And I was just sorta, kinda, well, you see I was just thinking and wondering and maybe even kinda hopin' that ... well, would you like to go with me to the ball?

BEAUTY: Are you asking me for a date?

UGLY GUY: *(unsure and rambling)* Well, yes I am. Would you like to go with me? I mean, I realize that I'm certainly one of the ugliest and strangest and most repulsive creatures you've ever seen. And I'm probably not a very good dancer or anything like that. And I can barely carry on a conversation with anyone. And sometimes I have bad breath and really gross people out when I talk with them. And I'm sorta clumsy and will probably spill punch and cookies all over you. And I never take a bath and probably smell like I've been living in a sewer all my life. And I never comb my hair or brush my teeth. And my clothes are all dirty and torn and beat up and ragged and stained and all that stuff. And I never clip my toenails or wash my socks. But in spite of all that, I've got a really great personality.

BEAUTY: Well, you know, I am sort of intrigued. I've never gone out with an extraordinarily grotesque and hideous guy before. It sounds like it might be fun. Okay, yeah, sure, why not? Let's go out.

UGLY GUY: *(excitedly)* Oh, wow! That's great. Look, why don't I pick you up in my beat-up, old hay wagon next Friday night at about seven. Okay?

BEAUTY: That sounds good. I'll see you then.

NARRATOR II: And so it was that this remarkably repulsive and unattractive guy was able to take the most incredibly ravishing and stunning maiden in the whole kingdom to the annual Fall Ball. And, of course, they had a great time ... except when the really monstrous and unsightly guy tried to kiss the wonderfully and exquisitely beautiful young maiden. But that's another story.

THE REALLY, REALLY, <u>REALLY</u> TRUE STORY OF THE THREE LITTLE PIGS

STAGING:

The narrator is at a lectern or podium near the front of the staging area. The three pigs are on stools or chairs. The wolf is standing and moves back and forth among the other characters.

Very Smart Pig	*Average Pig*	*Not Too Bright Pig*
X	X	X

Mean and Grouchy Wolf
X

Narrator
X

NARRATOR: A long time ago, when fairy tales used to be inhabited by animals who could talk and think, there lived these three pigs. Yeah, yeah, yeah, I know what you're saying—each of them built a house and along came this mean old wolf with incredibly bad breath who blows down the first two houses because they weren't built according to the local zoning laws and then tries to blow down the third house, which is, incidentally, made of reinforced concrete, not bricks, and he eventually falls into a big pot of boiling water and the three pigs live happily ever after, at least until their mother finds out what they've been doing and sends them to bed without their dinner. Well, that's probably the story you heard when you were a tiny tyke, but that's not the really real story. Actually, your parents couldn't tell you the really real story 'cause it was filled with all kinds of violence and a couple of bad words. Well, now that you're all grown up and very mature, we're going to tell you the really, really, <u>really</u> true story of the Three Little Pigs—but, of course, we're going to have to leave out all those bad words.

25

So, anyway, one day these three brothers who, as you know by now, were pigs—and, as you also know, they were talking pigs—were sitting in the living room of their mother's four-bedroom condominium reading some of the latest issues of *Better Pigs and Gardens* and the *New Porker*. And that's where the really, really, <u>really</u> true story of the Three Little Pigs begins.

VERY SMART PIG: Hey, brothers, you know it's about time we moved out of Mom's house. We're grown up now and ready to go out into the world to seek our fortune. And besides, Mom's getting on in years and won't be able to support us much longer. In fact, pretty soon we're going to have to think about putting her in the Old Porker's Home.

AVERAGE PIG: You know, brother, you've got a point there. Besides, we wouldn't have much of a story if all we did was sit around Mom's living room discussing the color of her drapes or "500 Uses for Bacon Bits."

NOT TOO BRIGHT PIG: Yeah! It sure is getting crowded in here, too. You know, because we're pigs we don't clean up after ourselves, so we track mud all over the place, and we make funny grunting noises for most of the day. I think the neighbors are beginning to wonder what we really do. We better move out while we still can.

NARRATOR: And so it was that the three brothers decided to move out of Mom's house and buy some property in the country. The real estate agent assured them that the land was ideal—rolling hills, lots of space, and no strange or weird animals in the nearby forest.

MEAN AND GROUCHY WOLF: *(insulted)* Hey, wait a minute! Aren't I supposed to have a place in this story, too?

NARRATOR: *(forcefully)* Hey, keep your shirt on! We'll sneak you over from the Red Riding Hood story, and no one will be the wiser. In fact, if you play your cards right, you can finish this story and get back to Grandma's house in time to hop back into her pajamas and wait for that naive Riding Hood girl to come along.

MEAN AND GROUCHY WOLF: Okay, okay. But make it quick, buster. You know what the wolf's union says about me doing double time.

NARRATOR:	Anyway, as I was saying, the three pigs began to build their dream houses along the country road that ran through their property.
NOT TOO BRIGHT PIG:	You know, I'm not very smart, so I think I'll build my house out of straw. So, who cares if it blows down in the first windstorm of the season or leaks like a sieve in the winter.
MEAN AND GROUCHY WOLF:	*(insulted)* Hey, now hold on a minute! Do you honestly think I would want to waste my time with that little porker? You know, I've got far better things to do with my time than wait until that not too bright pig builds his weak, little house of straw for me to come prancing down the lane to huff and puff and blow it down. That's got to be an absolute waste of my finely tuned acting talents!
NARRATOR:	Well then, what if we move this story along and see what Average Pig does.
MEAN AND GROUCHY WOLF:	Well, okay, but this better be a lot more interesting than that little ham bone with the pile of hay in his backyard.
NARRATOR:	Settle down! Don't have a coronary! Just let me see what I can do with this part of the story. It's all yours, Average Pig.
AVERAGE PIG:	Thanks. While you guys were talking I was walking around my property gathering some sticks and branches and tree limbs. I think I'll build my house out of this stuff. It may not be too sturdy, but at least it won't fall down the first time I slam the front door. Of course, the local fire marshal may have a thing or two to say about it.
MEAN AND GROUCHY WOLF:	*(angrily)* Now just a gosh darn minute here! You want me to believe that this walking pile of pork chops is really going to build a house of sticks so that I can come along and blow it down just like I was supposed to do with his brother's house? Come on, get real! I mean, what a waste! Why would I even want to take the time to huff and puff my way around this stupid little structure? You know, you guys are really starting to tick me off. All I can say is, this story better get a lot better and real fast, too!
NARRATOR:	Boy, you sure do get pushy. You know, this is supposed to be a story about the Three Little Pigs, not about some wolf with an attitude.

MEAN AND GROUCHY WOLF: Look, wise guy, how'd you like me to nibble on your face? If I want to take the lead role in this story, then I'm going to. After all, just look what my brothers and I have been putting up with in all those other stories.

NARRATOR: *(indignantly)* Now, just hold on. We still have to see what Very Smart Pig does with his part in the story.

VERY SMART PIG: You know, they don't call me Very Smart Pig for nothin'. In fact, I'm the guy they call on to bring home the bacon ... get it? Bring home the bacon! So, while this hotshot wolf was thinking about huffing and puffing down some flimsy houses built by my two less than brilliant brothers, I was constructing a house completely out of bricks and steel and reinforced cement. Ain't nobody going to blow this baby down! I mean this beauty is built!!! And any wolf who has any kind of smarts would do well to just keep his distance. I mean we're talkin' SOLID here!

MEAN AND GROUCHY WOLF: *(very angrily)* Look, I'm not takin' any gruff from some lard-faced pig. I'll huff and puff my way across the whole county if I want to. I'll blow down, damage, and destroy as many houses as I want.

VERY SMART PIG: *(angrily)* Yeah, you and whose army?

MEAN AND GROUCHY WOLF: *(angrily)* Hey, watch it, pork breath. How would you like me to turn you into a pile of ham sandwiches?

VERY SMART PIG: *(very angrily)* Yeah, just go ahead and try it.

MEAN AND GROUCHY WOLF: *(extremely angry)* Just watch me.

NARRATOR: All day long Very Smart Pig and Mean and Grouchy Wolf argued about who was the strongest and who was the smartest. In fact, Wolf and Pig went far into the night with their argument, and for all we know they're still arguing away. But, of course, that would never make for an exciting story for the kiddies. So a long time ago a bunch of fairy tale writers got together and decided to spice up the story a bit and turn the wolf into a door-to-door salesperson with an asthma problem. The rest, as they say, is history. And now, you know the really, really, really true story of the Three Little Pigs.

THE BRUSSELS SPROUTS MAN
(The Gingerbread Man's Unbelievably Strange Cousin)

STAGING:

The narrator can sit on a stool to the front and side of all the characters. The characters may wish to sit in chairs or stand, depending on the amount of space available.

Gingerbread Man	*Fudge Ripple Ice Cream Man*	*Lemon Meringue Pie Man*	*Chocolate Chip Cookie Man*
X	**X**	**X**	**X**

Brussels Sprouts Man
X

Little Girl	*Little Boy*
X	**X**
Fat Cow	*Clever Fox*
X	**X**

Narrator
X

NARRATOR: *(somewhat dejectedly)* Even before we get started with this story, I'm going to be honest with you. One of the characters behind me is really gross! And I mean GROSS!!! He's not your typical fairy tale character or handsome prince in shining armor type. He's not even someone you'd want to invite home to spend the night. He's weird, he's strange ... he's just totally gross. Actually, the only reason we're doing a story about him is that his agent made a deal with some other fairy tale characters that we wanted to use in some future stories, and this guy just became part of the package. It wasn't anything we did on purpose, but we really wanted to get those other stars so we were forced to use him. We hope you'll understand.

29

(more excitedly) Now, once upon a time in a far-off land and a far-off place there lived this incredibly gross individual known as the Brussels Sprouts Man. Actually, not too many people knew about the Brussels Sprouts Man, but they had heard all the stories about his more famous cousin, the Gingerbread Man. Well, as it so happens, one day the Brussels Sprouts Man decided to visit his cousin, the Gingerbread Man, and all the Gingerbread Man's relatives—the Fudge Ripple Ice Cream Man, the Lemon Meringue Pie Man, and the Chocolate Chip Cookie Man.

GINGERBREAD MAN: *(excitedly)* Hey, look who's coming for a visit. It's my very strange cousin, the Brussels Sprouts Man.

FUDGE RIPPLE ICE CREAM MAN: *(disgusted)* Whew! Are you gross. Where did you get that awful taste, that awful smell, and those awful green things all over your body?

BRUSSELS SPROUTS MAN: *(sadly)* Hey, look guys. It's not my fault that my parents just happened to be some old broccoli stalks and Ping-Pong balls. That's just the way I am.

CHOCOLATE CHIP COOKIE MAN: Have you ever considered hiding out in a cave for the rest of your life? You know, you're starting to give the whole family a bad name. All the kids really like us, but if they were to ever find out that you were related to us, well, our reputations would be shot.

LEMON MERINGUE PIE MAN: *(sarcastically)* Yeah. We've worked hard to achieve places of honor in the food chain. After all, we represent three of the four major food groups—sugar, starch, and sweets.

GINGERBREAD MAN: Now look, cousin, we're about to take a walk down this path to see if we can outwit some other characters for this story. You're welcome to tag along, but please don't admit you know us, okay?

BRUSSELS SPROUTS MAN: Okay.

NARRATOR: And so it was that the five companions set off down the road. As you might imagine, this wasn't just any road—it was a road of destiny! Just watch.

FUDGE RIPPLE ICE CREAM MAN: Hey, look guys. There's a Little Boy, a Little Girl, a Fat Cow, and a Clever Fox waiting for us down the road — just like in that other story. Let's be real careful now, because you know what might happen.

ALL CHARACTERS: *(together)* Right.

LITTLE GIRL: Hey, now here's a sweet-looking group.

LITTLE BOY: Yeah, but who's your weird-looking friend?

GINGERBREAD MAN: Why, that's my cousin, the Brussels Sprouts Man.

FAT COW: *(disgusted)* Oh, gross! How did he hook up with you guys?

CHOCOLATE CHIP COOKIE MAN: Well, you know how these stories are. You're just never sure who's going to show up.

CLEVER FOX: *(winking)* Well, then, what do you say we get on with this story. I believe that at this point in the story you're supposed to sing some kind of tune that will get us irritated enough to want to chase you down the road. But, on second thought, we can probably make this a true short story if we just ate all of you right now. Believe me, I'd love to run after you, but to be perfectly honest, after a couple hundred of these fairy tales over the years my body is just not as fast as it used to be. So I think we'll just grab you and eat you all right here in the middle of the road. That is, all of you except your weird little green friend there.

NARRATOR: And so it was that the Little Girl grabbed the Fudge Ripple Ice Cream Man, the Little Boy grabbed the Lemon Meringue Pie Man, the Fat Cow grabbed the Chocolate Chip Cookie Man, and the Clever Fox grabbed the Gingerbread Man, and they all sat down in the middle of the road and ate them all up. Of course, nobody wanted to eat the Brussels Sprouts Man. So, he just continued walking down the road singing.

BRUSSELS SPROUTS MAN: *(singing happily)* Sit, sit, sit on your can. You won't eat me, I'm the Brussels Sprouts Man. Sit, sit, sit on your can. You won't eat me, I'm the Brussels Sprouts Man. Sit, sit, sit on your....

THE BIG _____ WOLF AND THE DAY HE FORGOT HIS MIDDLE NAME

STAGING:

The narrator stands in front of the audience. The wolf stands and moves back and forth across the stage from character to character. The other characters sit on stools or chairs.

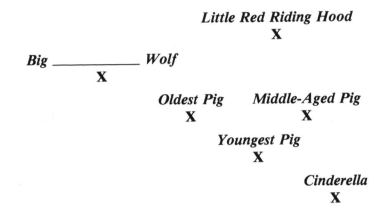

Little Red Riding Hood
X

Big _____ Wolf
X

Oldest Pig   *Middle-Aged Pig*
X   X

Youngest Pig
X

Cinderella
X

Narrator
X

NARRATOR:	This is a sad story.
ALL CHARACTERS:	*(together)* A-w-w-w-w-w-w-w-w-w-w-w-w-w-w!
NARRATOR:	No, really, it's a very sad story, perhaps not one to put tears in your eyes, but a sad story nonetheless. It's about a character you usually find in a lot of those old-time fairy tales—you know, the stories about little children who go off into the woods without telling their parents, or stories about a character with a bad attitude who wants to do nothing else but eat some of the other characters, or at least scare them to death. Well, in this case, our main character is a wolf. Now before you go saying that this is probably just an average, everyday wolf who lives in the heart of the forest waiting for a good meal to come along, let me explain something. You see, this wolf has a problem.

ALL CHARACTERS: *(together)* A-w-w-w-w-w-w-w-w-w-w-w-w-w-w!

NARRATOR: Now stop that! Seriously, this wolf has a major problem. For you see, this wolf has forgotten part of his name. Actually, the part of his name he has forgotten is in the middle of his name, which is why he's known as the Big ___(blank)___ Wolf. But, enough of my talking, I'll let him tell you.

BIG _____ WOLF: Honestly, I don't know how it happened. I just woke up one day and completely forgot part of my name. The only thing I know is that part of my name is supposed to be an adjective and that particular adjective describes my behavior, my character, and my personality. In other words, if I don't know what my middle name is, I won't know how to behave in a story. And I won't know how to act with other characters. You can imagine how confusing that would be. *(turning)* Oh, excuse me, little girl. Could you please help me out?

LITTLE RED RIDING HOOD: Yeah, what is it, manure breath? Can't you see I'm on my way to Granny's house with some tuna sandwiches and chocolate milk? Waddaya want?

BIG _____ WOLF: You see, I've completely forgotten my middle name, which means I've also forgotten how to act with little girls who skip through the forest with a basket of goodies for their grandmother who lives in a cottage in the middle of the forest. And if I don't know my middle name, then I don't know how I'm supposed to act with you. For example, if my middle name was Silly, then I could just stand here and tell you some jokes like the one about the cow who tried to jump over the barbed wire fence but didn't quite make it. It was an udder disaster. Get it? An *udder* disaster.

LITTLE RED RIDING HOOD: *(short-tempered)* Look, cut to the chase, buddy. I haven't got all day. Just what is your point?

BIG _____ WOLF: Well, I'm confused. I still haven't been able to figure out my middle name. If it's Smelly, then that means I wouldn't have to take any more showers and could get as stinky as I wanted. Of course, no one would want to have me in any stories. If my middle name was Strong, then I could spend all day in the forest beating up all the rabbits and foxes who just happen to walk by.

LITTLE RED RIDING HOOD: *(angrily)* Look here, you big fur ball. I haven't got all day to listen to you. Why don't you go on over to the three brothers who live over in that next story. Maybe they can help you out. But, before you go, I would strongly suggest you brush your teeth. Whew!

BIG _____ WOLF: Well, what have I got to lose? *(walks over to the three pigs)* Say, brothers, do you think you could help me out?

OLDEST PIG: What do you mean, "help you out"? You must be kidding. After what you've done in all those stories to all those other characters, you expect us to just stop rolling around in the mud here and help you out? Just who do you think you are?

BIG _____ WOLF: Well, that's just what I'm trying to find out. You see, when I woke up this morning, I'd completely forgotten my middle name. It was gone, vanished, disappeared, kaput! Now if I don't remember what that name is, I'll never be able to figure out how to act toward you guys or any of the other characters in any of the other stories with wolves in them.

MIDDLE-AGED PIG: Hey, I know what his name is. It's Stupid. Yeah, that's it. It's Stupid. You're the Big Stupid Wolf. Yeah, and all you get to do in these stories is have people drop buckets of water on your head and play all kinds of practical jokes on you all day long.

BIG _____ WOLF: Gee, do ya really think that's my name? It doesn't sound too familiar, but you've been in these stories before so maybe you do know.

YOUNGEST PIG: No, no, no. I know what your middle name is. It's Goofy. Yeah, you're the Big Goofy Wolf. You spend all day hanging upside down in trees. You prance around the yard like a chicken. You jump out of airplanes without a parachute. You make faces at all the animals who pass through the forest. You eat your food with your feet. Yeah, yeah, yeah. Your middle name is Goofy.

BIG _____ WOLF: Do you really think so? Gosh, it doesn't sound all that familiar, but maybe you're right. I guess I could try it for a while to see if it works.

OLDEST PIG: No, no, his name is Weird. He's the Big Weird Wolf. Ha, ha, ha.

YOUNGEST PIG:	No, it's Crazy.
MIDDLE-AGED PIG:	How 'bout Dopey?
OLDEST PIG:	No ... Invisible.
YOUNGEST PIG:	Lazy.
MIDDLE-AGED PIG:	Sleepy.
CINDERELLA:	How about Handsome?
OLDEST PIG:	*(to Cinderella)* Say, how'd you get in our story anyway? Don't you belong in another story?
NARRATOR:	Well, as you see, no one was able to help out the Big _____ Wolf. He just went from story to story, asking all the characters what they thought his name was. And, of course, no one was able to tell him his real name because, you see, they weren't very bright story characters either.

HANSEL AND GRETEL MAKE A REALLY BIG MISTAKE WITH THEIR NEW FRIEND FROM ANOTHER STORY

STAGING:
The narrator sits on a high stool in front of the audience. Each of the three characters stands.

Gretel   *Hansel*   *Gingerbread Man*
X   X   X

Narrator
X

NARRATOR: If you've been following our stories so far, you probably know that some really weird things sometimes happen to storybook characters and those strange people who are found in fairy tales and such. Sometimes these characters are really dumb, like the prince who goes around to every swamp in town to kiss as many green amphibians as he can, hoping, of course, to find the love of his life. Then there are the characters who skip through forests filled with dangerous wolves and other mean creatures, thinking they can make it to Grandma's house without some kind of accident. Anyway, as I was saying, these stories have your usual assortment of stupid characters and strange-looking beings.

Now, once upon a time there were two children who lived with their evil stepmother and their sensitive father deep in the big, big forest. One day they just got tired of doing all the chores their evil stepmother made them do, like washing the car, vacuuming the rugs, doing the dishes, painting the aluminum siding on the house, and repairing the air conditioning unit. So they decided to leave home, journeying, of course, through the heart of the deep, dark forest. (Why is it that these characters never live in a condo in the suburbs?) But you've probably heard enough from me already, so I'll just let them tell their story....

GRETEL: Hey, Hansel, how 'bout you and me taking off through this incredibly deep and extremely dark forest to see if we can find out what's on the other side of this story?

HANSEL: Sounds good to me, sis. By the way, do you have any idea what kind of creatures or wicked witches the writer is going to have us meet up with?

GRETEL: I've no idea, but we're already well into this story so I guess we'll just have to continue on down this path to find out what he has in mind for us.

HANSEL: I sure hope we don't have to walk past that mucky, dismal swamp that has all those frogs in it waiting to be kissed by every fair maiden in the county. That would really slow down the story.

GRETEL: Right. So let's get a move on!

NARRATOR: Hansel and his fantastically beautiful and undeniably brilliant sister went skipping down the path that winds through the deep, dark forest. It wasn't too long before they met another character from a different story.

HANSEL: Hey, look, it's the Gingerbread Man. Hey, Gingerbread Man, what are you doing in this story?

GINGERBREAD MAN: I don't know. The last thing I remember was crossing a river on the back of this supposedly intelligent fox. The next thing I know I'm waking up on the bank of the river with the fox sound asleep beside me.

GRETEL: Boy, that's not how I remember the story.

GINGERBREAD MAN: Me neither. I think the story was supposed to end with me being eaten by the fox. But that's okay, I guess this writer has decided to give me another chance.

HANSEL: That's okay with us, too. Say, would you like to join us as we skip down this path through the deep, dark forest? We think that somewhere down here there's a wicked witch who wants to eat us up. Maybe you could help distract her while we hit her over the head with a shovel. Then we could change the ending of the story or maybe even invent a new story.

GINGERBREAD MAN: Okay.

NARRATOR: So it was that the three companions skipped on down the path through the deep, dark forest. It was just a little while later that Gretel made a seemingly innocent remark that was to forever change the direction of the story.

GRETEL: Hey, it's almost noon and I'm getting really hungry.

NARRATOR: A short time later Hansel and Gretel arrived at the cottage of the wicked witch, but without their gingerbread companion. To this day no one knows what happened to the Gingerbread Man, even though the F.B.I. has launched an intensive Gingerbread Man hunt. Hansel and Gretel have refused to answer any questions and have referred all inquiries to their attorney. The case is still open. Anyone with information on the whereabouts of the Gingerbread Man is asked to call the authorities immediately.

DON'T KISS SLEEPING BEAUTY, SHE'S GOT REALLY BAD BREATH

STAGING:

The narrator stands off to the side. The characters can each sit on a separate stool or chair, or they can stand in a circle in front of the audience, too.

Narrator
X

Prince #1	*Prince #2*	*Prince #3*	*Prince #4*
X	**X**	**X**	**X**

NARRATOR: Now here's another story that also happened a long time ago. I guess that's just the way it is with fairy tales. They all seem to take place in the "good old days" — you know, the days before microwave ovens and cellular telephones. Anyway, once upon a time, there was this incredibly beautiful princess who was so good-looking that all the princes from miles around wanted to marry her. Every time she walked down the street, all the princes would stand around with their tongues hanging out of their mouths just hoping to get a look at her. She was one gorgeous lady. Now, in order to make this story somewhat interesting, we have to have an evil character, and as is usually the case, the evil character in this and other stories just happens to be a wicked witch. (Gee, it sure does seem like there's an awful lot of wicked witches running around fairy tales, doesn't it?) In this story, the wicked witch gets the incredibly beautiful princess to eat some kind of semipoisoned food that makes her immediately fall into a deep sleep. However, the witch makes the mistake of tossing the poison bottle in the town garbage dump. One of the princes finds it and notices that the antidote to the poison is a kiss from a handsome prince.

PRINCE #1: Wow! All I have to do is kiss Sleeping Beauty and she will awaken from her sleep to be my bride.

NARRATOR: *(to the prince)* That's right, Prince #1.

NARRATOR: *(to the audience)* Obviously, this guy isn't playing with a full deck. But anyway, let's jump ahead to when Prince #1 returns to the castle to tell his prince friends about his adventures.

PRINCE #1: Hey, guys. You're not going to believe this, but that Sleeping Beauty woman is sound asleep in that small cottage at the edge of the enchanted forest just waiting for one of us to stop by and give her a kiss that will wake her up.

PRINCE #2: Well, why didn't you kiss her?

PRINCE #1: Well, it seems as though our fair maiden has bad breath.... I mean really bad breath! It was so bad that all the flowers in the house had wilted and the wallpaper was peeling off the walls. WHEW! Boy, did it stink!!!

PRINCE #3: You mean, you didn't kiss her after all?

PRINCE #1: No way, José. I couldn't even get in the room. I mean, even the flies were dropping like flies!

PRINCE #4: That's unbelievable. Here's this incredibly gorgeous princess, sleeping like a baby in the cottage just down the road, and we can't even get close enough to kiss her. Wow, what a waste!

PRINCE #1: Yeah, and just as bad is the fact that she snores like a bear. Every time she breathes the windows rattle and the dishes in the kitchen crack and break. You'd have to be crazy to want to live with a woman like that. Not only will her breath make your skin peel, but her snoring is enough to wake the dead.

PRINCE #3: Boy, that's unbelievable!

PRINCE #1: If you think that's bad, you should see what all the animals in the forest are doing. They're packing up and leaving in droves. Not only is she stinking up the air, but she's making the whole neighborhood shake with her snoring. It's getting to the point that nobody wants to be within five miles of the small cottage at the edge of the Enchanted Forest.

PRINCE #2: Well, how are we going to wake her up? Doesn't somebody have to kiss her, marry her, and live happily ever after in order for this story to end the right way?

PRINCE #1: Hey, maybe you pal ... but not me! If you want to go ahead and kiss old Hog's Breath, then help yourself. As for me, I'm going over to the next forest and see if I can get a date with Snow White, that is, if she's not going out with Grumpy, or Sneezy, or Dopey, or someone.

NARRATOR: And so it was that nobody wanted to kiss Sleeping Beauty. It wasn't until many years later, when mouthwash was invented, that a traveling salesman finally had the nerve to pour some Scope mouthwash into Sleeping Beauty's mouth. He kissed her and she finally awakened. But, of course, she couldn't marry him because he was no Prince Charming. So she spent the rest of her life living in the forest with a few squirrels and talking to lizards.

THE INCREDIBLY STUPID PRINCESS
WHO WANTS TO PUT LOTS
OF VEGETABLES
UNDER HER MATTRESSES

STAGING:

The narrator stands to the side and behind the other characters. The characters can sit on stools or stand to one side of the room.

Narrator
X

                     Princess   *King*   *Queen*   *Prince*
                        X   **X**   **X**   **X**

NARRATOR: Once upon a time there was this princess. Now it should be mentioned that this particular princess was not the brightest kid you ever met. She probably had a lot of things rattling around in her head, and one of those things certainly wasn't an oversized brain. Anyway, this princess who, incidentally, was a little on the ugly side, thought it was time that she should snare herself a rich and handsome young prince and settle down to raise a family.

           Now, as it happened, this not-very-bright and not-very-good-looking princess had been to the public library and had read the story about the princess in another kingdom who was able to marry a gorgeous prince simply because she was able to feel a pea under one hundred mattresses the night she had stopped by his castle for a visit. So, this somewhat stupid and very unattractive princess had an idea that she thought might get her a dashing prince, too. Our story begins outside a large and impressive castle—the home of the incredibly rich and incredibly good-looking prince.

PRINCESS: *(happily)* Well, here I am at the first castle on my list. I've got all my mattresses and a whole bushel basket full of vegetables just like that other princess. So, let's see what happens. *(rings the doorbell)*

KING: Oh, hello, you not-so-bright and not-so-beautiful princess. How can I help you?

PRINCESS: Well, King, you see, I'm looking for a very handsome and very rich young prince to marry, so I thought I'd stop by your castle to see if I might be just the thing for your dashing young son.

KING: Well, what do you have in mind?

PRINCESS: Well, I thought that I would pile my one hundred mattresses on top of each other and then put a couple of green vegetables under them. If I woke up in the morning with a backache, then that would prove that I was a worthy bride for your incredibly handsome and fantastically rich young son.

QUEEN: Just a minute. Don't you have this backwards? In the original story, aren't we supposed to supply the one hundred mattresses and then secretly slip a pea beneath the bottom one to see if you would feel it while you slept? And if you did, then that would mean that you were a true princess, and hence a worthy bride for our wonderfully handsome and powerfully rich son?

PRINCESS: Look, I read that story just like you did, but I thought I might jazz it up a bit. First of all, I'm saving you the trouble of hunting all over the kingdom for one hundred mattresses. I just happen to have one hundred here in the back of my carriage. Also, I brought along my own vegetables to sleep on. Now, anybody can sleep on a pea, but what if I were to sleep on a bushel of asparagus, a crop of corn, a load of sweet potatoes, a truckload of beans, and a couple of crates of lettuce? That would make that other princess look like some kind of wimp, now wouldn't it?

PRINCE: That's true. But don't you think that the vegetables should be put under your mattresses secretly by my parents? After all, if you knew what kinds of vegetables were under your mattresses before you went to sleep, then you'd be able to force yourself to have a lousy night's sleep just so you could marry handsome me.

PRINCESS: *(indignantly)* Would I do something like that? My only goal is to show that little mousy princess in the castle down the street that a *real* princess is one who can sleep on any kind of vegetable.

KING: It seems to me as if you're trying to set the rules for this story. We know you're not very bright and certainly not very pretty because the narrator told us so. But this little scheme of yours is stupid, dumb, and ridiculous and would only make us the laughing stock of the whole kingdom. I'm sorry, but we can't help you out.

QUEEN: Have you tried that new family that just moved into the vacant castle next door? Their son is not as handsome and certainly not as rich as ours, but who knows, he might be just what you're looking for.

PRINCESS: Thanks anyway.

QUEEN: *(closing the door)* You know, I'm not too sure why she was put into this story. She's not very smart and certainly not very pretty.

PRINCE: Yeah, how'd she get to be a princess anyway?

KING: I guess her father just happened to know the right people.

PRINCE: Maybe so, but I sure hope she doesn't show up in another story like this in the future.

QUEEN: Hopefully, the writer will turn her into an evil stepsister and use her in one of those Cinderella stories. After all, she's really very ugly and really very dumb, you know.

LITTLE RED RIDING HOOD AND THE BIG BAD WOLF HAVE A FRIENDLY CONVERSATION (Finally)

STAGING:

The narrator sits far behind the two characters. The characters can stand in front of the audience or sit on two tall stools. Little Red Riding Hood uses a play telephone.

                                                                                    Narrator
                                                                                        X

        Little Red Riding Hood   *Big Bad Wolf*
                 X   **X**

LITTLE RED RIDING HOOD: *(happily)* Hi, my name's Little Red Riding Hood, and I'm the star of this story. First of all, let me explain something to you. You'll probably notice that the narrator is sitting way back there *(she points)*. We thought about it for a long time and decided that a narrator really wasn't necessary for this story. It's not that we don't like narrators—they're actually pretty nice—it's just that we felt like giving the narrator a rest in this story and doing it ourselves.

So, anyway, this is the story of how I listen real carefully to my grandmother before I go to visit her on the other side of the forest. It's also about a meaningful conversation I have with the Big Bad Wolf—the same guy who used to harass little girls and break into old people's homes. But this time around he's a whole new individual! Just watch.

LITTLE RED RIDING HOOD: *(talking on the telephone)* That's right, Granny. I'll be real careful when I come to visit you. I'll look both ways when I cross the street, I won't talk to any strange creatures along the way, and I'll make sure I leave home in plenty of time to arrive at your house before dark. Oh, and yes, I'll be sure to carry a can of Mace with me, too. Bye, bye, Granny. I'll see you soon.

44

NARRATOR: *(to audience)* You know, I was just thinking. This story just isn't going to work out like it should if there's no narrator. So, if it's all right with you guys, I think I'll just jump in here and see if I can help this story along.

(to audience) By now you know that Little Red Riding Hood is off on her visit to Granny's house. And you also probably know that she's going to meet the Big Bad Wolf along the way. So let's get back into this story and see how Little Red Riding Hood handles herself in the forest.

LITTLE RED RIDING HOOD: *(singing to the tune of "It's a Beautiful Day in the Neighborhood," [a.k.a., "Mr. Rogers' Neighborhood" theme song])* It's a beautiful day for a forest walk, a beautiful day for a forest walk, we should watch out, we should watch out, we should watch out for strangers.

BIG BAD WOLF: Hey, little girl, what are you doing?

LITTLE RED RIDING HOOD: Obviously you're not too bright, wolfman. You must be familiar with this story by now. Can't you see that I'm on my way to Granny's house?

BIG BAD WOLF: Oh, yeah, right! I guess I kinda forgot. You know, it's been such a long time since I've been in this story.

LITTLE RED RIDING HOOD: So anyway, fur face, what have you been up to lately? *(to audience)* Now look, don't be too surprised at my attitude toward this guy. He's just a wolf, not your usual story creature with long teeth and blood dripping down his face. It's not like this guy is scary or anything. He's just a wolf. A big dumb wolf. Certainly nothing to get excited about.

BIG BAD WOLF: *(to Little Red Riding Hood)* Well, you see, I've been spending time with my brother lately trying to get him to a doctor. You probably met him in another story ... he's the one with asthma. Yeah, whenever he gets around straw or sticks or even bricks, he feels like he's got to huff and puff. It's really cutting down on his social life and certainly making the local police quite suspicious of his actions. I'm trying to get him some allergy tests, but so far I haven't been too successful.

LITTLE RED RIDING HOOD: Well, the next time you see your brother, please give him my best. I think that with a little medical help, he might be able to control his heavy breathing and begin to assume a more normal lifestyle—like killing defenseless sheep and stuff like that.

BIG BAD WOLF: Yeah, thanks, I'll tell him you said "Hi." By the way, what have you got in your basket there?

LITTLE RED RIDING HOOD: Oh, just a couple of new CDs for my granny, a few MTV videos, and some chocolate chip cookies. You know how lonely it can get out there in the middle of the forest. So I thought I'd bring along some entertainment to help her pass the time. Say, how would you like to do me a favor?

BIG BAD WOLF: Name it.

LITTLE RED RIDING HOOD: Well, as you know, Granny is awfully lonely. She doesn't get many visitors—you know what a bad reputation this forest has. Would you mind dropping in on her every once in a while? Nothing special, just a friendly visit. Of course, there can't be any funny stuff like in the last story—no putting on her pajamas or eating her up. Those things really bother her.

BIG BAD WOLF: No problem. I'd love to drop in and chat. It gets pretty lonely in the forest for us animals, too. After all, all I usually get to do is eat a few rabbits, growl a little, and sleep for most of the day. I'd love to be able to visit Granny every so often. She's good company.

LITTLE RED RIDING HOOD: Then it's done. I guess I'd better be on my way now. Granny will be expecting me. And because you're not going to eat me or my granny in this story, I don't have to worry about you anymore. But maybe I'll see you the next time I'm through these woods.

BIG BAD WOLF: Yeah, take care. Hope to see you soon!

NARRATOR: Unbelievable. I guess the Big Bad Wolf has finally turned over a new leaf. From now on, it looks as if he's going to be a productive member of society and an outstanding citizen of the forest. It may even change the outcome of other fairy tales, too. I'll call the Three Little Pigs next week and let you know what I find out.

THE THREE BILLY GOATS GRUFF DON'T WANT TO BOTHER WITH THE TROLL SO THEY EAT AT PIZZA HUT INSTEAD

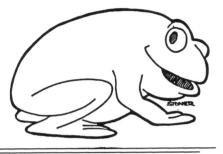

STAGING:

The narrator stands at a lectern. Each of the three goats stands. The troll sits in the background on a high stool.

```
                                              Troll
                                                X

        Biggoat      Mediumgoat      Smallgoat
           X             X               X

Narrator
   X
```

NARRATOR: Once upon a time there were these three goats who stood around on a hill eating grass all day long. Obviously, they weren't very bright. I mean, who in their right mind would knowingly want to stick their face in the dirt and mud so they could chew on some yucky old grass that they had been walking on the day before. Anyway, as so often happens in these kinds of stories, one of the goats gets an idea. Now, admittedly, it's not the most brilliant idea you've ever heard, but if you want to find out how this story turns out you'll have to listen to it. So, here goes.

MEDIUMGOAT: *(dejectedly)* Hey, I don't know about you guys, but I'm sure getting tired of standing around on this stupid hill all day long eating nothing but grass and walking around in this stupid mud. I mean, are we dumb, or what?

SMALLGOAT: *(sarcastically)* You got that right, pal! It's not much of a life to stand around on this hill with some dumb cows and a couple of sheep who wouldn't know a good meal if it hit them in the face. After all, what do we have to look forward to in life—more grass, more pastures, more mud, and more neighbors? What a waste! Don't you think it's about time we got a life?

BIGGOAT: *(somewhat excitedly)* Listen, brothers, we have it made. We can go to work anytime we want. We can eat whatever and whenever we want. We can stroll around this pasture at will. And while I must admit that the cows next door aren't the smartest animals on four legs, they're harmless and certainly haven't caused us any problems since we moved here.

MEDIUMGOAT: Yeah, but you're always supposed to say that. You're the big brother, and in most stories like this you're supposed to be the smartest.

SMALLGOAT: *(forcefully)* Besides eating nothing but muddy grass, I'm also getting just a little tired of having to deal with that ugly old troll who lives under the bridge that leads to the meadow next door. I mean that guy is so ugly he has to wear a paper bag over his head just to look at himself in the mirror. And to top it off, he smells! Whew!

MEDIUMGOAT: *(excitedly)* You know, Small is right. Every time we want some good grass shoots to nibble on for an appetizer or whenever we want to have a tasty snack of turf, that ugly old troll stops us at the bridge to ask some silly question like "Who's trampling on my bridge?" It certainly doesn't take a rocket scientist to see that we look like goats, walk like goats, talk like goats, and even eat like goats. Who else does he think is going to be crossing that bridge—Cinderella and her two ugly stepsisters?

BIGGOAT: You guys are probably right. But just remember that the troll is not the smartest guy around. After all, anyone who lives under a bridge can't be all that bright. On the other hand, let's consider this guy's social life. With his incredibly awful breath and bad manners, how many birthday parties do you think he gets invited to, how many rock concerts does he get to go to, and how many Fourth of July picnics do you think he attends? Other than us, he doesn't associate with anyone. In fact, if it wasn't for us trying to cross the bridge every week or so, the troll would have no social life at all. When you think about it, we're really doing the guy a favor.

NARRATOR: *(to the audience)* As you know, ladies and gentlemen, in the fairy tale business it's the big brother who always gets the best lines. Now, this one may not be the brightest goat you've ever seen, but because he's so much older than the others, let's humor him a little by letting him have some of the better lines. Okay?

TROLL: *(shrugging his shoulders)* Hey, don't look at me. I'm just some ugly troll minding his own business. Of course, the real question you should be asking is why a bunch of intelligent people like yourselves would want to sit around and listen to a bunch of talking goats. Think about it.

MEDIUMGOAT: Well, I don't know about you guys, but frankly, all this talk about grass and pastures and meadows is making me hungry. What do you say we look for some other place to eat today, a place that doesn't have trolls, or bridges, or a bunch of silly cows chewing their cud all day long.

SMALLGOAT: *(excitedly)* I'm with Medium. I'm getting hungry, too. But I'm really not hungry for more grass. I bet if we strolled on down to the mall on the corner of the south pasture we'd find a couple of fast food places that served something a little more exciting than grass and clover. In fact, come to think of it, I could really go for a large pizza with mushrooms and pepperoni.

BIGGOAT: Yeah, that sounds good to me, too. You know how long it's been since we've had anything decent to eat? After all, in every other version of this story all we do is cross some stupid bridge and talk with some stupid troll just so we can eat some stupid grass. Now that's stupid! I say it's about time we take charge of this story and get some real food. I'll tell you, a Whopper, a Pan Pizza, or some Chicken McNuggets sound awfully good right now. And if you go through the drive-up window, you don't even have to deal with any stupid ugly trolls.

MEDIUMGOAT: *(really excited)* You know, a couple of chocolate shakes, large fries, and a few apple pies *do* sound good! What do you say, guys? Let's go.

NARRATOR: And so it was that the three Billy Goats Gruff strolled on down to their neighborhood pizza parlor to order a couple of large pizzas with extra cheese and three medium root beers. When they discovered that Pizza Hut delivered directly to their pasture they totally freaked out! So it was that three talking goats, who used to eat nothing but grass and an occasional tin can or two, were able to fill up on Pan Pizzas and bread sticks for the rest of their lives. And they never had to worry about the troll again.

TROLL: *(dejectedly)* Oh, that's just great! And do you think Pizza Hut delivers to trolls under bridges? N-o-o-o-o-o-o-o-o. Just because I have to live under some stupid bridge in some stupid pasture, I can't get pizza delivered. Those dumb goats get sausage and pepperoni and mozzarella cheese, and all I get to eat is a bunch of stupid pasture grass. Thanks a lot! Just see if I show up in another one of your weird stories.

NARRATOR: Well, not all of our tales can have "happily ever after" endings.

JACK CLIMBS TO THE TOP OF A VERY TALL VEGETABLE AND FINDS A VERY LARGE INDIVIDUAL WITH AN ATTITUDE PROBLEM

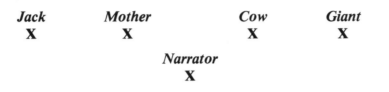

STAGING:

The narrator sits on a stool in front of the characters. The characters can sit in chairs or stand.

Jack	Mother	Cow	Giant
X	X	X	X

Narrator
X

NARRATOR: You all probably remember the story about Jack and his encounters with a former NBA basketball player who just happened to live at the top of a very tall bean plant. Now the writers who told you that story would have you believe that this very tall person who lived at the top of the very tall bean plant had nothing better to do with his time than eat unsuspecting little boys who just happened to climb to the top of that very tall bean plant looking for gold to take home to their poor, starving mothers who lived around the bottom of that very tall plant. Well, it is true that giants are known far and wide for their ability to nibble, chew, and chomp on little boys. However, the version of that story you heard is not the real story—the real story is the one that you're going to hear right now.

JACK: *(excitedly)* Hey, Mom, guess what I did. I went down to the marketplace with our cow, Bessie, and sold her to this nice used car salesman for a handful of cactus seeds.

NARRATOR: *(to the audience)* You've probably guessed that Jack is not the brightest kid around. For, as everyone knows, you can't get cactus seeds from a used car salesman. But, after all, this is a fairy tale, so why don't we all just pretend?

MOTHER: *(angrily)* You silly boy! What do you mean you traded our best cow, in fact, our only cow, for a handful of stupid seeds from some used car salesman.

COW: *(to audience)* Yeah, think how I feel. I've just spent the last ten years of my life giving this family some of the best milk ever produced in six counties, and this dumb kid just hauls me off to the marketplace, gets taken in by a smooth-talking salesman, and trades me for a bunch of cactus seeds. Talk about feeling bad!

MOTHER: *(still angry)* Jack, you take these useless cactus seeds, go back down to the marketplace, find that salesman, and get our cow back.

JACK: *(lightly)* Okay, Mom, I'll do it first thing tomorrow. In the meantime, why don't you just throw these seeds out the window and let's see what happens.

NARRATOR: I'm sorry, folks, but we're going to have to stop the story right here. In the first place, because these folks live in the mountains there's no way those cactus seeds are going to sprout. As you know, cacti (that's the plural of cactus) only grow in hot, dry areas such as deserts. In the second place, imagine what would happen if that cactus actually *did* grow one thousand feet tall. I mean, don't you think Jack would have a really tough time trying to climb to the top of that enormous plant? Talk about getting stuck in a story! It looks like your friendly neighborhood narrator is going to have to save the day once again and change some of the dialogue so that we can continue on. So, here goes.

JACK: *(amazed)* Oh, how amazing. Those useless cactus seeds have magically turned into bean seeds. Gosh, isn't that narrator amazing?

MOTHER: Yes, and now I can throw those bean seeds out the window and we can continue on with this story.

NARRATOR: Mother throws the bean seeds out the window, a beanstalk about five thousand feet tall grows during the night, and now it's the next morning.

JACK: *(excitedly)* Wow! Unbelievable! Incredible! Out of sight!

MOTHER: What are you mumbling about now, my dear son? *(looks out the window)* Hey, holy moley, will you take a look at that enormous beanstalk. That must be the biggest thing since Billy Bob grew that incredible sunflower in the manure pile outside his barn last summer.

JACK: *(eagerly)* Well, Mother, time is wasting. This is a short story, so I better get moving and climb up this beanstalk to see what's at the top. I sure hope I don't run into any giant problems while I'm there!

NARRATOR: Jack begins to climb up the beanstalk. After several days, he arrives at the top only to be greeted by an enormous person with bad breath and an attitude problem — what you and I would refer to as a giant.

GIANT: *(angrily)* Hey, what makes you think you can just climb up any convenient beanstalk and come into my yard. I should have you arrested and hauled off to jail.

JACK: Hey, look, Mr. Giant, I'm just following directions. The writer of this story said that I should climb up this beanstalk, sneak into your castle, run away with your golden harp and your hen that lays those incredibly golden eggs, and then live happily ever after with my mother.

GIANT: *(very angrily)* Say, who is that writer anyway? Just wait until I get my hands on him!

JACK: So, do you mind if we continue on with this story?

GIANT: *(extremely angrily)* Mind! You bet your little pinhead I mind. In fact, I'm getting sick and tired of all you little creeps climbing up all these beanstalks to bother me and my wife. Just look at this place. There's potato chip bags, candy wrappers, and little pieces of bubble gum left all over the yard. It's one thing to come visiting without being invited and quite another to be complete slobs and leave all your garbage around here. The least you could do would be to clean up after yourselves. This place is beginning to look like a dump.

JACK: *(meekly)* Hey, look, this is just my first visit — actually it's my first story with you. I'm not like all those other guys in all those other fairy tales. Honest.

GIANT: Oh yeah? Well, if that's the case, then why don't you just pick up all this trash, mow my lawn, wash my windows, sweep the driveway, and paint the picket fence.

JACK: Oh, I think I hear my mother calling me for dinner. You'll excuse me.

GIANT: *(laughing)* Ha, ha, ha. That works every time.

NARRATOR: And so it was that Jack never got to steal the golden harp or run off with the hen that laid the golden eggs — those events were added by another writer. Some time later, Jack and his mother moved to Arizona and started a mail order cactus business. The giant, we hear, eventually sold his castle to some real estate developers, and he and his wife moved into a condo on top of another tall vegetable. And the cow, well, nobody knows what happened to the cow.

COW: *(dejectedly)* It figures!

CINDERELLA VISITS THE SHOE STORE AND GETS A PAIR OF AIR JORDANS

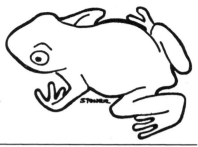

STAGING:

The narrator should be standing to the side of the two major characters. Cinderella and the shoe salesman can sit on tall stools or on chairs.

	Cinderella **X**	*Shoe Salesman* **X**
Narrator **X**		

NARRATOR: Once upon a long time ago there was this semi-princess — you know, the kind of princess who lived in this big ugly castle with her big ugly stepsisters and her big ugly stepmother. Every day this semi-princess, Cinderella (known as Cindy to her friends), would wash and wax all the floors in this big ugly castle while her big ugly stepsisters and big ugly stepmother would go to all the dances and parties throughout the kingdom (of course, nobody ever danced with these big ugly women simply because they were just *too* big and *too* ugly ... but they went to all the parties anyway). Of course, because Cinderella did so much washing and waxing of the floors, she would often run out of floor soap and floor wax and would have to visit her local supermarket to buy more. Well, this one day, while she was walking around the shopping mall, she happened to pass by a shoe store. She was looking in the window at all the shoes when she got this brilliant idea. So she went in.

CINDERELLA: *(excitedly)* Hey, Mr. Shoe Salesman! Do you happen to have any shoes that I could wear to the next ball at the local palace? You see, I'm hoping some tall, dark, and handsome prince will come along, sweep me off my feet, put me in his magic carriage, and carry me off to his enchanted castle in the next kingdom ... or something like that.

SHOE SALESMAN: Hey, hold your horses. You obviously don't know your fairy tales very well. Don't you know you've got to have some fairy godmother come along first to give you the finest dress in all the land and create a pumpkin with tiny horses to drive you to the local palace?

CINDERELLA: *(forcefully)* Look, get real! This is the new age. I'm going to get myself some of the latest fashions from Europe and really knock out all those princes hangin' around the castle tonight. I'll be so good lookin' that every prince in the place will want to dance with me. All I need is the right pair of shoes and I'll be the hit of the ball.

SHOE SALESMAN: Look, the object of the story is not to have the best-looking pair of shoes, but to have a pair of shoes that don't fit too well so that when you're running down the castle steps at the stroke of midnight, one of the shoes will fall off and be found by one of those tall, dark, and handsome princes who will race around the city the next day to try it on all the young ladies, except that you're the only one who can fit into the shoe so you're the one who gets to marry the lucky prince.

CINDERELLA: *(impatiently)* Listen, Jack! That may be your version of the story, but it's not mine. See, in my version of the story I'm the one in charge. I get to choose which prince I want to dance with, and if he's no good, then I'll just drop him like a ton of bricks. Frankly, I'm tired of playing second fiddle to all these guys in all these fairy tales who get most of the action and most of the good lines. You know, now that I think about it, I think it's high time we fairy tale women get equal billing in these stories. It's about time we get the major roles, the major movie contracts, and the major bucks for doing these stories. For too long we've been taking it on the chin, storywise, and now we're going to stand up for our rights. *(excitedly)* Yeah, yeah, yeah! In fact, let's forget about those fancy-dancy Italian pumps, those fancy-dancy parties at the castles, and those fancy-dancy princes with their noses stuck so far up in the air that they're getting nosebleeds. I'm changing my mind. After all, this is MY story. You know what I'd really like to have, instead of some stupid dancing shoes, is a pair of Air Jordans. *(forcefully)* And while I'm thinking of it, why don't we just forget about this whole palace ball and prince thing, too? What I'd really like to do is take on a few of those hotshot princes in a game of one on one. Let's see if those fancy-dancy princes can shoot some three-pointers and make a couple of slam dunks. Yeah, they haven't seen nothin' yet.

SHOE SALESMAN: Well, if you say so. If you'll wait just a moment I'll get a few pairs of Air Jordans from the back.

NARRATOR: And so it was that Cinderella totally forgot about the palace ball and the stupid princes who had nothing better to do with their time than run around the village testing some high heel slippers on some of the smelliest and stinkiest feet in the whole county. Meanwhile, Cinderella was off organizing her own summer basketball league with a couple of the characters from other fairy tales. Cinderella, along with Little Red Riding Hood, Rapunzel, Sleeping Beauty, and Snow White, eventually formed their own basketball team and whipped the socks off of every team that challenged them that summer. Later, Cinderella was approached by representatives of a major shoe manufacturer to create her own brand of sneakers. She eventually retired a very rich woman.

JACK AND JILL GO FETCH A PAIL OF WATER AND LATER DECIDE TO CHANGE THE NAME OF THEIR STORY (And By the Way, What Does the Word "Fetch" Mean Anyway?)

STAGING:
The narrator is seated on a tall stool. The characters can be standing or seated on tall stools.

```
                        Jack      Jill
                         X         X

Narrator                                                    Frog
   X                                                          X
```

NARRATOR: *(somewhat sarcastically)* Once upon a time there were these two kids — Jack and Jill by name. Now, I'll admit that Jack and Jill aren't the two most original names you've ever heard for nursery rhyme characters, but remember, this is a story from the old days, and they didn't have a lot of imagination back then. So please just try to bear with me. Anyway, as I was saying, these kids got themselves involved in this really stupid story about the two of them walking up to the top of this hill to get some water in a bucket and then walking down the hill again. I mean is that exciting, or what? Yeah, that's the whole story. Except, of course, I forgot the part where Jack, who isn't too coordinated, trips over his shoelaces and rolls all the way down the hill. Jill, because she wants equal treatment in this particular Mother Goose story, also decides to trip over her shoelaces and fall down the hill, too. Now aren't you *really* excited? I mean doesn't that sound like one of the most adventurous and thrilling stories you've ever heard? I thought so. Well, anyway, these two kids thought that the original story should be spiced up just a little bit (I wonder why). So here is their version of the Jack and Jill adventure.

JILL: Look, Jack. We can't go around telling people that we climbed to the top of a hill, tried to get some water, lost our balance, and rolled down to the bottom. I mean, what kind of stupid story is that?

JACK: Yeah, you're right. How many kids are going to get excited hearing about two klutzes who fall down and spill water all over themselves? I don't know about you, but that kind of story line sure wouldn't be at the top of my hit parade. What do you suggest we do?

56

JILL: Well, as I see it, I think we need to chuck the whole story and start from scratch. How about if we get chased by some evil wizard with a magic potion he wants to pour all over us to turn us into frogs or something disgusting like that?

FROG: *(indignantly)* Hey, just wait a minute. I resent that! This may be your story, but that certainly doesn't give you the right to pick on the characters from other stories. So just ease up!

JACK: Okay. That sounds like it might work, but doesn't it sound like all those other fairy tales and Mother Goose rhymes? How about if we are exploring the deepest, darkest jungle when all of a sudden we are attacked by a giant human-eating bird that lives at the top of a flesh-eating tree on the edge of a great smelly swamp? As we're running away, we lose our balance and roll into the mouth of an erupting volcano, where we are slowly covered by a carpet of molten lava. Of course, because all Mother Goose stories have to have happy endings, we'll have to be saved by some handsome prince or a half dozen or so dwarfs.

JILL: Yeah, but that happens in all the stories. Why can't we just look out for ourselves and go about saving our own skins for a change?

JACK: Well, okay, so what's your idea?

JILL: Maybe we could live in a far-off kingdom ruled by evil kings and queens, and our mother, the evilest of all stepmothers, could try to get us beheaded by the wicked wizard of the Eastern Forest, who just happens to collect the brains of little boys and girls.

JACK: No, I don't think that will work either.

JILL: *(resigned)* Yeah, it sounds like we've got a real story problem on our hands. Maybe we should just stay with the original version. It has less violence and blood and guts and gore and all that other stuff that parents don't want their kids to read about. It's safe and it's harmless. Sure, it's not the greatest story line, but at least it's held up over the years. We just get a few bumps and scratches and that's about it. No big deal.

JACK: Yeah, you're right. We'd better leave well enough alone.

NARRATOR: And so it was that Jack and Jill decided not to change their story ... except that Jill requested that the name of the story be changed to "Jill, and the Day Jack Pushed Her Down the Hill on Purpose."

RUMPLESTILTSKIN TRIES TO SPELL HIS NAME

STAGING:

The narrator stands off to the side of the staging area. The teacher and all the students can sit on stools or chairs in the middle of the staging area.

		Tom X	John X
Teacher X	Rumplestiltskin X		
		Mary X	Karen X

Narrator
X

NARRATOR: *(rambling)* Once upon a time in a far-off village in a far-off country in a far-off time there lived some far-off people. Well, they really weren't as far off as you might think, but it was certain that they were happy and contented individuals because they went around all day long with big fat smiles plastered on their big happy faces ... and they sang a lot ... and they hummed a lot ... and they whistled a lot ... and all that other kind of stuff that makes you sort of wonder if they've all been eating too many brussels sprouts or something. Anyway, one day in the school in that strange and weird village an incident occurred that has evolved into one of the most remembered fairy tales of all. Unfortunately, however, the version you know is not the right version. That version was put together by some fairy tale writers who wanted all the children to obey their parents, go to bed early, and keep their rooms absolutely clean—even on weekends. Sad to say, that's the version we all remember. But perhaps you might want to know the true incidents behind the tale that we know today. So, let's look in on that classroom in that strange and weird village and find out what really happened—or, at least, what should have happened.

TEACHER: Now, boys and girls, I'd like you to meet our newest student. He comes to us from far away, so he'll probably fit right in here with all the loopy people in our strange and far-off village. His name is Rumplestiltskin, and I hope you will make him feel welcome!

TOM: *(sarcastically)* Rumplestiltskin! Rumplestiltskin! What a weird name! Where'd you ever get a name like that?

RUMPLESTILTSKIN: Actually, my parents gave it to me. They got it from some wicked witch who found it inside a kettle full of bat brains, salamander tongues, and lizard eyes.

JOHN: *(facetiously)* What a joke! Do you mean to say that your full name is Rumplestiltskin? Why can't you have a normal name like Bruce or Larry or Carlos or John? What are we going to call you for short? Rumple? Rumpy? Rump? Hey, now there's a good one—look, here comes the Rump Man! Hey, ya big rump, why don't you put your big rump in your big chair? Ha, ha, ha, ha, ha.

MARY: Maybe we ought to call him Skin or Skinhead. Hey, ya big skinhead, where's your hair? Did some enchanted princess come along and take it away from you? Or did some handsome prince steal it for his own. Ha, ha, ha, ha, ha.

KAREN: No, maybe we should call him Stilts because he's s-o-o-o-o-o-o-o tall. Wow, he must be at least two feet seven inches tall … I mean, he's a really big, big man. I'm so-o-o-o-o-o-impressed. Ha, ha, ha, ha, ha.

TEACHER: *(sweetly and gently)* Now, boys and girls, don't you think we should show our new student some respect? *(now angrily and demanding)* In other words, get off his case!!!

JOHN: But, Teach, it's just that we've never heard such a strange and weird name before. I'd like to know how he spells it.

TEACHER: Well, Rumplestiltskin, could you please write your name on the chalkboard for us?

RUMPLESTILTSKIN: Sure. Let's see now, I think it's R-u-m-p-p-l.... No, no, no, that's not it. Let me try again. Maybe it's R-u-m-m-p-p-l-l.... No, that's not it either. How 'bout R-r-u-m-p-p-l-l-e.... No, I guess that's not it either. You know, I've never really learned how to spell my name. I guess it's just because most of us fairy tale characters have never been inside a real live classroom. *(rambling)* I mean, all we usually get to do is sit around some old forest waiting for the dumb people in the next town to come waltzing through, get lost and have to have some kind of meaningful adventure where they are saved by some enchanted prince or some strange men who work in a mine all day or maybe even a fairy godmother who rides around the countryside in a pumpkin or some other kind of vegetable with wheels on it. It's not like we haven't got anything better to do, it's just that those writers have us doing the same old things story after story. We never have any time to go to school, get a real job, drive a car, or all the other things that some story characters do. We have to spend our time with evil witches who have incredibly bad breath and wicked wizards who don't know their wands from a hole in the ground. It's not that we don't want to get more involved, it's just that we're never given a chance to get involved. I guess that's sort of a long-winded answer to why I've never learned how to spell my own name. I've spent so much time running around drafty castles and getting angry at airhead princesses that I've never had the time to learn to spell my name.

TEACHER: Well, boys and girls, I guess it's time we help Rumplestiltskin learn to spell his name. Maybe if we all work together we can figure this out. Let's see what we can do.

NARRATOR: And so it was that the class worked for days and days on the spelling of Rumplestiltskin's name. Obviously, they were not a very bright class, but they all pitched in to help out their new classmate. *(rambling)* But, it wasn't until an evil stepmother who had been turned into an enchanted frog by a wicked wizard and who lived by a mysterious pond full of fire-breathing dragons and other creatures with bad breath was able to cast her magic spell over the whole town that Rumplestiltskin and all his classmates were able to figure out the spelling of his name. But, of course, that's another fairy tale altogether!

RAPUNZEL GETS A REALLY LOUSY HAIRDO

STAGING:

The narrator stands to the side in back of the characters. The husband and wife stand; the other characters sit on tall stools in front of the audience.

Narrator
X

                                             Husband   *Wife*
                                                 X   X

        Witch   *Rapunzel*   *Maurice*
         X   X   X

NARRATOR: A long time ago, when there were all kinds of witches and princes and princesses (and, of course, some frogs) running around the fairy tales of old, there lived this couple. Behind the couple's house was an apartment complex where an old witch, who did nothing all day but count her social security checks and brew some foul-smelling stew, lived. Now, as is so often the case in these stories, the couple had a daughter who was more beautiful than anyone you'd ever see in the "Swimsuit Issue" of *Sports Illustrated*. Well, to make a long story short, the witch became tired of just counting her money and smelling up the neighborhood with her awful stew, so she decided to kidnap the beautiful daughter and put her up in the tower of an old castle that just happened to be on the edge of town.

HUSBAND and WIFE: *(together)* Oh, no!

NARRATOR: Each day the witch would visit the incredibly beautiful daughter in the tower and tell her to throw down her hair so the witch could climb up it and bring the daughter some food and some old magazines to read. Obviously, the daughter was not too bright because she never ever made any attempt to escape. Of course, if she did, we wouldn't have much of a story. But, anyway, now you've got an idea of the background for this tale, so I'll turn it over to the characters.

WITCH: *(loudly)* Hey, Rapunzel, how about turning off your CD player and tossing down your hair so I can climb up there with some breakfast for you. I've got a stack of pancakes, a side of bacon, some hash browns, a plate of scrambled eggs, a pot of coffee, and some freshly squeezed Florida orange juice today.

RAPUNZEL: Okay, here it comes.

NARRATOR: Rapunzel—her friends called her Rap—tosses down her hair, and the evil witch climbs up.

WITCH: Wow, is your hair ever dirty. When's the last time you washed it?

RAPUNZEL: Oh, two or three years ago, I guess. It was the day you kidnapped me and put me up in this tower.

HUSBAND and WIFE: *(together)* Oh, no!

WITCH: Boy, does it ever need some work. When I get back to the castle I'll call my hairdresser and ask him to come over to fix you up.

NARRATOR: Later that day, the witch calls up the local beauty parlor and makes arrangements for Maurice to visit Rapunzel and give her a shampoo, blow dry, style, and set. The next morning Maurice visits the tower.

MAURICE: Hey, Rapunzel, it's me, Maurice. How 'bout tossing down your hair so I can climb up to the tower and give you your permanent.

NARRATOR: Rapunzel tosses down her hair, and Maurice climbs up.

MAURICE: Wow, is your hair ever dirty. What have you been doing with it?

RAPUNZEL: I just toss it down each day for the evil witch to climb up. Other than that, I just let it grow.

MAURICE: Well, let's see what we can do with it. You know, you'll never be able to win over that handsome young prince in the next castle if you don't wash your hair.

NARRATOR: Maurice worked on Rapunzel's hair for most of the morning. Unfortunately, Maurice was getting old, and his eyesight wasn't very good. By the time he was done with Rapunzel's hair, it looked as though a bunch of squirrels had built a nest in it. In fact, when Rapunzel looked in the mirror she screamed—a scream that could be heard in every castle in the neighborhood.

HUSBAND and WIFE: *(together)* Oh, no!

RAPUNZEL: What have you done? My hair is ruined! I'll never get that handsome young prince in the next castle to come over here to rescue me. You've ruined my life. Get out! Get out! Get out!

NARRATOR: And so it was that Rapunzel spent the rest of her life in the tower in the castle on the outskirts of town. None of the princes ever came to visit her, much less rescue her. Even the evil witch ignored her and never asked her to let down her hair again. Rapunzel became a lonely and frustrated woman and soon began talking to all the spiders and other animals in the tower. She grew old and nobody ever invited her into any other story. It was a very sad ending for the former beauty contest winner.

HUSBAND and WIFE: *(together)* Oh, no!

THE BIG BAD WOLF GOES TO THE DOCTOR TO FIND OUT WHY HE CAN'T HUFF AND PUFF ANYMORE

STAGING:

The narrator should be seated on a stool in front of the audience. The other characters should all be standing. The wolf may move across the staging area during the course of the story.

Dr. Doolittle   *Big Bad Wolf*
X   X

Cinderella   *Hansel*
X   X

Gretel   *Snow White*
X   X

Goldilocks
X

Pharmacist
X

Narrator
X

NARRATOR: Once upon a time there was this wolf. Now, as you might expect, this was *the* Big Bad Wolf, but you'd never know it. See, the Wolf was having some real medical problems, breathing problems to be exact. He wasn't able to huff and he wasn't able to puff. In fact, he couldn't even blow out one candle on his birthday cake. So finally he decided it was time to go to the doctor to see what could be done.

DR. DOOLITTLE: Good morning, Mr. Wolf. What can we do for you today?

BIG BAD WOLF: Well, you see, Doc, I'm having some real breathing problems. Every time I visit someone's house I try to huff and I try to puff, but nothing happens. Nothing, not even a whisper. Now I'm really starting to become worried. In a few months I'm going to be in a story in which I'm supposed to blow down these houses belonging to these three little porkers, and I don't even have enough breath to whistle.

DR. DOOLITTLE: Well, well, well. We can't have that, can we? What would everyone say if the Big Bad Wolf couldn't even blow down a house made of straw? You'd probably be the laughingstock of all the fairy tale characters for miles around. Let's take a look down that throat of yours. Say "A-h-h-h-h-h."

BIG BAD WOLF: A-h-h-h-h-h-h-h.

DR. DOOLITTLE: H-m-m-m-m-m-m-m. I think I see the problem. It looks like you've got something stuck in your throat. I can't operate on it, but I can give you this prescription for some medicine that should take care of it.

BIG BAD WOLF: Do I have asthma, or bronchitis, or emphysema, Doc?

DR. DOOLITTLE: No, it's nothing as serious as that. It's just that you have a little something down in your throat that's causing you all those breathing problems. If you just get that medicine I prescribed, then you should be fine. Come back in a week or two, and we'll see how you're doing.

BIG BAD WOLF: Thanks, Doc. See ya around.

NARRATOR: Big Bad Wolf leaves the doctor's office and walks over to the drugstore on the other side of the forest. Along the way he has to pass by several characters' houses.

CINDERELLA: *(sarcastically)* Hey, guys, look. It's the Big Bad Wimp. Oh, *excuse me*, I meant the Big Bad Wolf. Ha, ha, ha. Having a little trouble huffing and puffing, Wolfie? Ha, ha, ha.

HANSEL: Hey, you big fur ball. I bet you couldn't even huff and puff your way out of a paper bag. Ha, ha, ha.

GRETEL: Hey look, guys. Look at Mr. Big Shot now. Why he's so big and mean and strong that I bet he could probably beat up a squirrel or a chipmunk or some really dangerous creature like that. Ha, ha, ha.

SNOW WHITE: What a wimp! How does it feel now, you overgrown river rat? You just think you can waltz into any story, scare and eat up all the characters, and live happily ever after? Fat chance. Ha, ha, ha.

GOLDILOCKS: *(sarcastically)* Yeah, I bet even Little Baby Bear could beat you up with both paws tied behind his back. Ha, ha, ha. Well, how does it feel, dog breath?

NARRATOR: And so it was. One character after another made fun of the not so Big Bad Wolf as he journeyed to the drugstore to get his medicine.

BIG BAD WOLF: Here, can you fill this prescription for me?

PHARMACIST: Hey look, guys, it's the old blowhard. He wants some medicine so he can huff and puff his way through some more flimsy houses. Ha, ha, ha.

BIG BAD WOLF: *(short-tempered)* Look, wise guy, just fill the prescription.

NARRATOR: The pharmacist fills the prescription, and the Big Bad Wolf takes it home. A week later he's back in the doctor's office.

DR. DOOLITTLE: Well, well, well. Don't you sound a lot better today!

BIG BAD WOLF: *(excitedly)* The change is amazing, Doc! I can huff and I can puff and I can blow down almost every house in the entire neighborhood. I feel great. I can hardly wait to get back into that story with those stupid three little pigs and really do some damage to their homes. Say, by the way, what was it that was stuck in my throat?

DR. DOOLITTLE: Actually, it was some of Granny's pajamas that you swallowed during the Little Red Riding Hood story. In the future, just stay away from flannel nighties and you'll be okay.

A BIG ROUND GUY FALLS OFF
A HIGH WALL AND CAUSES
QUITE A RUCKUS IN THE TOWN

STAGING:

The narrator should be standing near the front center of the staging area. The other characters can be standing or can be sitting on tall stools.

Reporter I   *Mike Raphone*
X   X

Sergeant Copper
X

Mary Merry
X

Mayor
X

Reporter II
X

Reporter III
X

Narrator
X

NARRATOR:	Once upon a time there were these three bears who....
REPORTER I:	*(interrupting)* Excuse me, buddy. But this just came in. We take you now to a wall just outside of town where our correspondent, Mike Raphone, is standing by. Come in, Mike.
MIKE RAPHONE:	Thanks. We're standing here by this large and long wall that just happens to be on the outskirts of town. No one knows why it's here, but it's the scene of one of the most gruesome scenes I've ever experienced in my twenty-four years in this business. Let's talk to Sergeant Copper of the City Police for an update. Tell us, Sergeant, what exactly happened here?
SERGEANT COPPER:	Well, it seems as though this big round guy just climbed to the top of the wall and threatened to jump off. He just sat there and kept yelling, "The yolk's on you, Copper, the yolk's on you!"

MIKE RAPHONE: What do you think he meant?

SERGEANT COPPER: Well, we have all our key people working on it right now. But that's not the worst of it. You see, just as he was sitting there ... we're not sure how it happened ... maybe it was just a gust of wind, or he just lost his balance....

MIKE RAPHONE: Well, what was it?

SERGEANT COPPER: Well, for some unknown reason, he just fell off the wall and splattered all over the sidewalk. I mean, his brains were scrambled all over the place, runny stuff just poured out of him, and there were shell fragments scattered in all directions.

REPORTER I: *(excitedly)* Mike, we're going to have to break away. This just came into the newsroom. It seems as though the mayor is about to make a speech to the townspeople. We take you now, live, to city hall where Mary Merry is standing by. Come in, Mary.

MARY MERRY: We're standing here just outside City Hall where the mayor, Noah Lott, is about to address the ... oh, here he comes now. Let's listen in.

MAYOR: *(officially)* My fellow townspeople, we have a great tragedy on our hands. It seems as though a big round individual has just fallen off the wall that is outside of town. We have police officials there now and should have an update for you shortly. There is absolutely no need to panic.

REPORTER II: Excuse me, Mr. Mayor, but what is currently being done about this situation?

MAYOR: We have called in all the king's horses and all the king's men and hope to have the situation put back together again in no time.

REPORTER III: Do you have any leads, any breaks in the case?

MAYOR: At this moment, no. But rest assured, we will work day and night on this matter until it is solved. We have some of the most competent eggs-perts on the scene right now.

REPORTER I: Well, there you have it folks, the latest update direct from the scene. As soon as something else breaks, we'll have the information to you immediately. We now return you to our regularly scheduled program.

THE REALLY, REALLY, <u>REALLY</u> TRUE STORY OF CINDERELLA

STAGING:

The narrator can sit on a stool or stand at a lectern in the middle of the staging area. The other characters can sit on stools or stand. Cinderella can move back and forth across the staging area.

Incredibly Ugly   *Incredibly Ugly*
Stepsister #1   *Stepsister #2*
X   **X**

Incredibly Handsome
Prince
X

Narrator
X

Cinderella
X

Really Incredibly Ugly
Stepmother
X

NARRATOR: Once upon a time, a long, long time ago, there lived this king guy. And this king guy had a wife who was very pretty, and they both lived in a large castle place high above the Enchanted Forest. They also had this daughter person who was incredibly beautiful and also very smart — certainly a lot smarter than some of the prince guys who always used to hang around the castle hoping to take Cinderella (for that was her name) on a date through the Enchanted Forest. As you might expect, Cinderella wanted nothing to do with these guys, who all had the manners of pigs and the personalities of trolls. Well, all that certainly wouldn't make much of a story other than the fact that the princes kept calling Cinderella, and she just kept saying she wasn't interested.

Well, as was so often the case in those times, Cinderella's mother died from eating too many of those little hot dogs with the toothpicks that were served at one of the castle balls that they always used to have. This made the king very sad, so he decided to get himself a new wife. He

69

put an ad in the paper, and in no time at all he was married once again. The only problem was that his new wife was uglier than a wart hog and had the temper of a wounded gorilla. She also had a bunch of daughters (from a previous marriage) who looked as though their faces had been run over by a herd of elephants; they, too, had the personalities of slugs. Well, in no time at all, Cinderella was banished to the kitchen, where she had to scrub the floors twice a day, peel bags and bags of potatoes, and clean out the cat's litter box by hand. That's just about where our story begins, so let's listen in.

CINDERELLA: *(disgusted)* You know, I've just about had it!

NARRATOR: *(aside)* You probably know that in a lot of these stories the main characters talk to themselves. That's just the way it is. It certainly doesn't mean they're crazy or have been sitting out in the sun too long or anything like that. It just means that they talk to themselves. That's it. Anyway....

CINDERELLA: *(still disgusted)* As I was saying, I've just about had it. Who does this wicked stepmother think she is? I mean, she's certainly not the heroine of this story ... she's just some stupid old hag who has nothing better to do with her time than put me to work in the kitchen while she spends her day gazing into some enchanted mirror that tells her she's the most beautiful creature in the entire kingdom. If she believes that, I have some beachfront property in Arizona to sell her.

INCREDIBLY HANDSOME PRINCE: *(smoothly)* Say, Cindy, I was just cruising through the castle and wondering if you'd like to go with me to the castle dance Friday night. After all, I'm so incredibly handsome and such an incredibly good dancer, and I've got such an incredibly swell stagecoach with some incredibly stunning stallions....

CINDERELLA: *(irritated)* Look, buster, why don't you and your incredibly oversized ego beat it. The last thing I need in my life is some stupid prince with incredibly bad breath taking me to some incredibly boring dance at some incredibly smelly castle.

INCREDIBLY HANDSOME PRINCE: *(very indignantly)* Well, humph!

INCREDIBLY UGLY STEPSISTER #1:	*(angrily)* Hey, Cindy. What do you think you're doing talking to some incredibly handsome prince? You're supposed to be down on your hands and knees scrubbing the kitchen floor with an old dishrag and cheap detergent.
CINDERELLA:	*(equally angry)* Look, wart face, I don't need you telling me what to do with my life. It wasn't my choice that my father went out and married the first woman he saw and that that woman just happened to have two of the ugliest and stupidest daughters this kingdom (or any kingdom, for that matter) has ever seen. No wonder every mirror in this place is broken; one look by you and mirrors for miles around shatter into millions of pieces. The best thing you could do is put a paper bag over your head and go live with the three bears in the middle of the forest.
INCREDIBLY UGLY STEPSISTER #1:	*(very indignant)* Well, I never....
CINDERELLA:	*(snappily)* Hey, just take a hike and leave me alone.
INCREDIBLY UGLY STEPSISTER #2:	What seems to be the problem here? And why aren't you pushing that mop around the floor and peeling that enormous pile of potatoes in the corner?
CINDERELLA:	*(sarcastically)* Oh, great! Just what I need — some other rhinoceros-faced stepsister who thinks she can just stand around and tell me how to live my life. Just look at her; she walks into a beauty parlor and they have to fumigate it for a whole week after she leaves. And talk about your smelly feet! WHEW!!!
INCREDIBLY UGLY STEPSISTER #2:	Hey look, sister. You know the story line as well as we do. All you're supposed to do is clean out this castle while my ugly sister, equally ugly mother, and I get dressed to go to the dance down at the castle gymnasium. That's it! No lip! No talking back! No nothing! Just follow the script and do your job and the story will turn out just like it's been written.
CINDERELLA:	*(irritatedly)* Well, I'm sick and tired of how the story always turns out!

REALLY INCREDIBLY UGLY STEPMOTHER: Hey, let's cut the chatter here. You girls should be getting ready for the dance and you, Miss Cinderella, should be scrubbing and cleaning and peeling and all that other stuff. Nobody gave you the right to tell us what you should be doing. And if you think you can just get your animal friends or some stupid fairy godmother to help you out, you have another thing coming. Now quit lollygagging and get to work! Let's go, incredibly ugly daughters.

NARRATOR: *(soothingly)* As you've probably guessed by now, Cinderella really has a bad attitude. She's tired, she's grumpy, and she's had it with everyone telling her what she should do and what she shouldn't do. And she hasn't even had time to put on her makeup.

So, at this point in the story you probably expect that something magical will happen. The so-called fairy godmother will appear out of nowhere to create an incredibly smashing gown and an equally smashing carriage for Cinderella to ride in to the castle dance. In fact, that's the way most people remember the story. But that's not the true story ... it's the story you've heard all these years ... but not the true story. But maybe I'd better let Cindy tell you herself.

CINDERELLA: *(defiantly)* Well, thanks a lot, buddy! *(to audience)* Anyway, I really got fed up with all the jerks I had to deal with, and I certainly didn't want to go to any dance and have a bunch of clods step all over my feet all night long ... and who needs those stupid princes anyway? So after my incredibly ugly stepsisters and my incredibly ugly stepmother left for the dance, I decided to have some pizza delivered to the castle and sit around in my pajamas and read a bunch of romance novels. Really, that's all I did all night long. Now the writers who put together the story wanted a little more action, so they made up all that stuff about the stupid prince and me losing my stupid shoe and the stupid prince going around the stupid city the next day to try the shoe on all the stupid women in town to see if one of them would marry him. Now if you really want to believe that, go ahead. But the truth is that all I did that night was read some trashy novels and eat a whole pepperoni pizza. Really!

NARRATOR: And so there you have it, folks ... the really, really, really true story of Cinderella. Honest!

ANOTHER STORY YOU'LL FIND HARD TO BELIEVE, BUT IT'S ALL TRUE ... HONEST!

STAGING:

The narrator can be seated on a stool to the side of the staging area. The Little Pizza Man can be standing and the other characters can be seated on stools. The Little Pizza Man may move between the characters.

<pre>
              Little Old Woman   Narrator
                    X   X

                         Little Old Man
                              X

                                    Cow
                                     X

  Little Pizza Man   Horse
         X   X

                              Little Girl
                                  X

                    Little Boy
                        X
</pre>

NARRATOR: Once upon a time there was a little old woman and a little old man, and they lived all alone in a little old house in the middle of a little old forest that was in the middle of a little old country, and so on, and so on, and so on. Anyway, they didn't have any little boys or any little girls (probably because they were too little to have any little children). So one day, the little old woman decided she wanted to have a little child for her very own, so she made one out of some pizza dough she found in the back of her refrigerator. She put some tomato sauce all over its face, two pepperoni slices for its eyes, a little tiny anchovy for its mouth, some little tiny sausage bits for its buttons, and two pieces of green pepper for its shoes. She decided to call her little pizza creation Bernard (remember, this was the old days when story characters weren't as bright as they are today). She put Bernard on a large pizza pan and shoved him into the oven to bake at 425° for about fifteen to twenty minutes. And then she said to herself, "Now, I shall have a little boy of my own."

When it was time for Bernard to be done, she opened the oven door and pulled out the pan. Out jumped the Little Pizza Man (as we will now call him), and away he ran, out the door and down the street. The little old woman and the little old man watched Bernard run away, laughing and shouting out loud:

LITTLE PIZZA MAN: "Run! run! as fast as you can!
"You can't catch me, I'm the Little Pizza Man!"

LITTLE OLD MAN: *(tiredly)* You know, I'm just a little old man with little old legs and a little old body, and I'll be darned if I'm going to run after some snotnosed brat just because he thinks he's the hero of this story.

LITTLE OLD WOMAN: *(agreeing)* You're right. Why would we want to hurt ourselves chasing after some dough boy who thinks he's the greatest thing since Pizza Hut started making home deliveries. For about six bucks we can get another one downtown. After all, all I did was take some flour and water and other ingredients and make a Little Pizza Man to keep us company. If he wants to thank us by running away, well, let him. I'm not about to waste my time chasing through the country hoping he'll come to his senses and return home.

NARRATOR: And so it was that the little old man and the little old woman decided that it was just too much trouble to go chasing the Little Pizza Man over the hills and valleys of the country. So, they decided to stay home and drink lots of iced tea.

But the Little Pizza Man continued to run through the town and bother everyone with his little chant:

LITTLE PIZZA MAN: "Run! run! as fast as you can!
"You can't catch me, I'm the Little Pizza Man!"

NARRATOR: Pretty soon, the Little Pizza Man left the town behind and ran and ran and ran and found himself back in the country, where he came to a cow standing in a pasture eating a bunch of grass (as you know, cows aren't very bright so all they get to do in these stories is eat some grass and leave their calling cards all over the pasture). The Little Pizza Man called out to the cow:

LITTLE PIZZA MAN: "I have run away from a little old woman,
"And a little old man,
"And I can run away from you, I can!
"Run! run! as fast as you can!
"You can't catch me, I'm the Little Pizza Man!"

NARRATOR: Well, as you know, cows can't talk, so she just stood in the pasture chewing on her cud and staring at the Little Pizza Man. After a while the Little Pizza Man got the hint and continued running down the road. The Little Pizza Man ran on and on until he came to a horse in another pasture. The horse was just standing there not doing anything, so the Little Pizza Man called out to the horse:

LITTLE PIZZA MAN: "I have run away from a little old woman,
"And a little old man,
"A cow,
"And I can run away from you, I can!
"Run! run! as fast as you can!
"You can't catch me, I'm the Little Pizza Man!"

NARRATOR: Well, just like the cow, the horse didn't do anything simply because horses don't understand English and don't talk. They'd rather run around a pasture all day and chase flies. Once again, the Little Pizza Man finally figured out that the horse wasn't going to say anything, no matter how long he hung around. So the Little Pizza Man decided to move on, and so he ran on and on until he came to a little boy and a little girl playing in a field. He stopped and called out to them:

LITTLE PIZZA MAN: "I have run away from a little old woman,
"And a little old man,
"A cow,
"A horse,
"And I can run away from you, I can!
"Run! run! as fast as you can!
"You can't catch me, I'm the Little Pizza Man!"

NARRATOR: Well, as it so happened, the little boy and the little girl were really into their little game, and they didn't hear what the Little Pizza Man said to them. The Little Pizza Man thought that they didn't understand English, just like the cow and the horse, so he decided to keep running down the road. In a little while he saw a fox standing in the middle of the road. He stopped and called out to the fox:

LITTLE PIZZA MAN: "I have run away from a little old woman,

"And a little old man,

"A cow,

"A horse,

"A little girl,

"A little boy,

"And I can run away from you, I can!

"Run! run! as fast as you can!

"You can't catch me, I'm the Little Pizza Man!"

NARRATOR: Now, at this point in the story, you're probably expecting one of two things to happen. Either the Little Pizza Man is going to talk to the fox, the fox won't understand what he's saying, and the Little Pizza Man will continue running down the road. Or, the fox will be a very intelligent creature who will listen carefully to the Little Pizza Man and then walk over and eat him for lunch. Now, that's what you might expect to happen, but remember that this is the really true and original version of this story, so the ending is going to be different from the one you're used to or even the one you might expect. But, maybe I'd better let the Little Pizza Man tell you how this story really ended.

LITTLE PIZZA MAN: After I'd run into the cow and the horse and the little boy and the little girl and, of course, the fox, I began to feel a little self-conscious. I mean, after all, I was asking all these characters to chase after me, and all they were doing was ignoring me. I couldn't figure it out until I began to realize something—I really stunk. Think about it. My whole body was covered with anchovies and tomato sauce and green peppers and pepperoni slices and all kinds of other stuff. Would you want to talk with someone who smelled like the back of your mother's refrigerator? Of course not! So I decided that the only thing I could do was to take a shower and clean myself up. But, of course, you know what happened after I did that. I just wasn't the same anymore. My sauce was gone and so was my entire personality. So now I spend my life working part time for the Pillsbury Dough Boy as a stunt man for his commercials. But at least I'm happy. Really!

IN A LIVING ROOM IN A HOUSE IN MOTHER GOOSE ESTATES

STAGING:

The narrator stands at a podium. The other characters sit on chairs or stools in a semicircular pattern.

Snow White   *Goldy Locks*
X   X

Sleep N. Beauty   *Rapunzel*
X   X

Cindy Rella   *Red Riding Hood*
X   X

Narrator
X

NARRATOR: Our "Once Upon a Time" story today opens up, not in some distant castle or overgrown enchanted forest, but rather in the living room of Ms. Cindy Rella. You see, Cindy is a former storybook character who just got tired of the daily grind of always having to get dressed up and always having to go to some stupid ball and always having to dance with some stupid prince with the intelligence of a sack of potatoes and always having to chase after some coach that looked more like a pumpkin than a Corvette, and so on, and so on.... I think you get the picture. Anyway, Cindy and several of her friends decided to retire from the storybook business and move out to Mother Goose Estates and away from all the big bad wolves, evil stepmothers, and princes who couldn't dance their way out of a paper bag.

And so, as we begin our tale, Cindy and several of her fellow storybook companions are sitting in her living room talking about "the good old days."

GOLDY LOCKS: Hey, Cindy. Tell me, why did you finally decide to give up all that castle stuff and retire to the Estates?

CINDY RELLA: Well, I just got fed up with the same plot line over and over again. After all, what was I doing with my life? Every time someone would tell my story, I would have to go out and work for an evil stepmother and then have a fairy godmother come and give me a beautiful Ralph Lauren original dress and get into this ugly pumpkin coach to take me to some distant palace where I would have to dance with every handsome dude, excuse me, I mean prince, in the place and then lose my shoes so some out-of-work prince could try and make me believe I'd be the happiest woman around if he could just hold my feet and make me try on some old, smelly slippers he always carried around with him. I don't know about you, but that kinda gets old after a while. What about you, Goldy? Why did you leave?

GOLDY LOCKS: You know, I was getting just a little sick and tired of always being cast as the dumb blonde who can't do anything else but wander through some stupid forest waiting for some stupid bears to leave their stupid house so I can break in and eat their stupid cold cereal. The writer was probably some guy who thinks that blondes have nothing better to do with their time than skip around the forest all day long and eat stale oatmeal. What do you think, Sleep?

SLEEP N. BEAUTY: *(sarcastically)* Gosh, I sure had some exciting story lines. After all, I got to wander through the Enchanted Forest and eat a poisoned piece of fruit (probably from the school cafeteria) and fall asleep for twenty years and be awakened by a dashing young dude on his big white horse who gets to plant a big wet one on my lips to wake me up and carry me away to his overpriced castle in the suburbs. *(indignantly)* Yeah, like I've got nothing better to do with my time than have some jerk with bad breath try and kiss me and tell me he can make me the happiest woman in town! Yeah, right! I mean, let's get real here! Who says I need a man, anyway? After you marry them, all they do is sit around the castle drinking ale and burping and expecting you to clean up after them all day long. So I decided to check out and open up my own business in the city. I'm not getting any younger, you know! Hey, what about you, Snow?

SNOW WHITE: I'm sure you heard about all the things I had to do in my story. Who the heck do those writers think they are, making me live with a bunch of real short men who think that the only thing I'm good at is picking up their dirty socks and sweeping their filthy pigsty of a house. Like I really enjoy spending my days sweeping and dusting and vacuuming and washing till these guys come home so I can cook them some barbecued chicken and homemade mashed potatoes. Now where is it written that the only thing we women are capable of doing is cleaning up after a bunch of slobs who track mud all over the floor and burp at dinnertime? I've certainly got better things to do than be a housemaid for seven jerks with bad manners. It didn't take too long before I just got sick and tired of the whole mess, packed my bags, and moved to Miami Beach, where I bought an apartment building for over-the-hill kings and princes. Now I'm really making some big bucks! Hey, Rapunzel, tell me, when did you decide to check out of the storybook scene?

RAPUNZEL: Well, for me, the decision was easy. Those jerks who wrote my story thought that I, too, was nothing more than some dumb blonde who really enjoyed a bunch of stupid princes using my hair as a staircase to climb up and down the castle walls. After a couple thousand of those episodes, as well as a couple thousand trips to the beauty parlor to repair my split ends, I decided it was high time I took charge of my own life. That's when I began to develop my own line of shampoo and hair conditioner products. I set up my own advertising agency and began marketing throughout the kingdom. Now I'm on easy street, and those jerky princes who used to climb up and down my locks are sitting around their castles all day long catching flies and boring themselves to death. I really became sick of all the men in all those stories having all the fun and getting all the best lines. So now, let's just see how they like it when they're left on their own in those smelly old castles! *(all the characters cheer)*

RED RIDING HOOD: Hey, you know what I think? I think that most of those original stories, which were obviously written by some guys who wouldn't know an intelligent woman if they met one, were just another way of showing how men think they have all the answers. Look at my case, for example. What was I expected to do but have a conversation with some fur ball in the forest who would then run to my granny's house, wait for me to come inside, and think that I was dumb enough to believe that he was my grandmother just because he was wearing her underwear. And, then, to top it all off I was supposed to be saved by some strong and muscular hunter who just happened to be wandering through the forest. Like Sleep said, let's get real here! I'd like nothing better than to blast that wimpy wolf into the next forest and dress up that stupid hunter in Granny's pajamas, and go out and get some pizza and PARTY HEARTY! *(all the characters cheer a little louder)*

GOLDY LOCKS: Well, ladies, I think we've made our case! Those stupid male writers have had their say for all these years. Now I think it's about time we made our voices heard. What do you think about striking for better lines, more intelligent roles, more money, and some creative freedom in our own stories?

ALL: Yeah! Yeah! Yeah!

NARRATOR: And so it was that all the female storybook characters began to design better stories and better plots for those stories. They became heroines and queens (without kings) and began a much needed revolution in fairy tales and legends. And all those male writers who used to write those stories about dumb women were left to write cute little stories about bunny rabbits and talking animals and stupid kings. And that's the truth!

Part III

HOP ON OVER—
HERE'S A BUNCH OF
FROG STORIES

THE FROG PRINCESS
(And What About All Those Frog Princes?)

STAGING:

All the characters, including the narrator, should stand or sit in a straight line or row in front of the audience.

Narrator	Wicked Witch	Frog Princess	Frog Prince	Frog	Fly	Toad
X	X	X	X	X	X	X

NARRATOR: Once upon a time there lived a frog princess. Now, before I go any further with this story, I'd better explain something. If you've read any fairy tales lately, you probably know that all those other fairy tales have nothing but frog *princes* in them. And you also know that each and every one of those frog princes was turned into an amphibian by an evil, mean, and ugly witch who had a chip on her shoulder or who was probably having a bad day. And, of course, you also know that those frog princes spend a good deal of their story time sitting on flimsy lily pads at a local swamp sticking their tongues out at passing flies and hoping that some sweet young princess will come along, give them a big smackeroo, and turn them back into the young, dashing, and handsome princes they once were. And, as always, the young, dashing, and handsome prince and the sweet, young princess ride off into the sunset on a white stallion to get married and live happily ever after. Well, that's how it usually happens, but you see, somewhere along the way with this story, something went wrong. But maybe I'd better let the characters explain it to you.

WICKED WITCH: *(dejectedly)* Look, it's not my fault that this story has a frog princess in it. Actually, my boss wanted me to increase my quota of frog princes this month, so I shifted my broom into high gear and cruised over to the kingdom's finest castle—the one swarming with all kinds of hunks ... er, excuse me, I mean filled with all kinds of princes—and decided to cast a spell on a few of them. Just as I waved my super-charged wand near a couple of them, this clueless princess walks right in front of me and, of course, gets turned into a frog. Hey, I can't help it if some dumb blonde is in the wrong place at the wrong time. I'm just trying to do my job.

FROG PRINCESS: *(angrily)* Boy, is that ever a bunch of baloney! All I was doing was dancing with this really neat prince guy who had just moved into town when the next thing I know my skin is green, I'm chasing some flies down the hall, and I've got this slimy gunk all over my body. Talk about gross! Just wait until my lawyer hears about this. That stupid witch will think twice about waving any magic wands around this castle again.

FROG PRINCE: Well, I guess it had to happen sometime. After all those stories in which my fellow princes and I are turned into wart-faced amphibians, it just seemed likely that someday one of the fair damsels would get caught in a wicked witch's spell and have to join us here in the mud. In fact, it's about time. I mean, shouldn't there be equality for all—princes and princesses, frogs and frogettes?

FROG: *(happily)* Actually, to be quite honest with you, I kind of like the idea. After all, it can get a little boring down here in the swamp when all you have to talk to are some princes who think they're pretty hot stuff just because some wicked witch turns them into frogs. Actually, most princes don't know diddley about being a frog. It's kind of refreshing to have a frog princess here in the bog. In fact, I kinda like the idea. Perhaps, with a little bit of luck, we'll be able to get some more frog princesses down here. Then we'll really be able to PARTY HEARTY!!!

FLY: *(sarcastically)* I don't know about you guys, but it really doesn't make much difference to me whether we have frog princes or frog princesses or even some plain old frogs down here in the swamp. Any way you look at it, they're all big, ugly, green amphibians with long tongues. The fact that they know how to say "thank you" and "please" and can blow their noses doesn't impress me one bit. What this swamp doesn't need is more frogs with attitude problems.

TOAD: Hey, don't look at me. I'm just happy for the company.

NARRATOR: And so that was the start of a change in the castle swamp. One by one, more and more young ladies were turned into frog princesses. And one by one, more princes from the nearby castle journeyed down to the swamp each day to kiss a couple of the frogs in hopes that they just might find the frog ... er, excuse me, I mean, girl of their dreams. Of course, sometimes those princes (who weren't always the brightest guys on two feet) would kiss one of the toads by mistake, but then, that's another story.

THE SEMICONFUSED PRINCE WHO LIVED IN A VERY LARGE CASTLE BY A BIG CRUDDY SWAMP FILLED WITH FUNNY GREEN AMPHIBIANS

STAGING:

The narrator stands in back and to the side of the other characters. The other characters may stand or may sit on high stools.

Semiconfused Prince	Wicked Witch	Frog #1	Frog #2	
X	X	X	X	
				Narrator
				X

NARRATOR: Once upon a time there was this semiconfused prince who lived in a very large castle by a big cruddy swamp filled with funny green amphibians. (Well, what did you expect—after all, that *is* the title of this story!) Anyway, as I was saying, this prince was somewhat confused. How confused, you might ask? He was so confused that he always rode his horse backwards so he could see where he had been. He was so confused that he thought that if he could get a frog to kiss him then he would become enchanted and would be able to marry the richest and most beautiful woman in the kingdom. Now, that's really confused. But I'm getting ahead of my story. Let's look in on this semiconfused prince and some of the semiconfused things he does. As you might expect, our story begins in the swamp.

SEMICONFUSED PRINCE: *(slowly)* Well, here I am again sitting on this lily pad. I sure do hope some enchanted frog comes along to kiss me so we can live happily ever after.

WICKED WITCH: *(shouting)* Hey, Prince!

SEMICONFUSED PRINCE: *(confused)* Say, where did you come from?

WICKED WITCH: Hey, you can't really be *that* dumb. You know, there's always some kind of wicked witch in stories like these. We just happen to be there.

SEMICONFUSED PRINCE: *(slowly and thoughtfully)* Yeah, now I remember. That must mean that you've got a whole pocket full of evil spells and magic sayings. How about tossing one my way?

WICKED WITCH: Now why would I want to do that? If I'm going to put a spell on anyone, at least it's going to be on a prince with some smarts. After all, I've got a reputation to maintain. If I cast a magic spell on every prince I meet, then there's no telling how many enchanted frogs we'd have hopping around these stories. Say, why do you want a spell, anyway?

SEMICONFUSED PRINCE: Oh, I don't really want a spell. What I want is to have you cast a spell on one of these lovely frogs hopping around the swamp so that when I kiss it, it will turn into a lovely princess whom I can carry off into Happily Ever After Land.

FROG #1: *(defiantly)* Now hold on just a minute, buster! What makes you think that you can have a spell put on one of us just because it's convenient for you? Hey, we've got a life to live, too. Just because a couple of my relatives show up in a few of these stories doesn't necessarily mean that all of us want to become enchanted.

FROG #2: *(defiantly)* Yeah! And anyway, isn't the wicked witch supposed to just cast her spells on princes and turn them into frogs who wait for desperate princesses to kiss them?

WICKED WITCH: *(smugly)* Hey, just a minute. Who do you think you are, telling me whom I can cast my spells on? After all, if I want to cast my spell on an amphibian rather than a human being, well, I'm certainly entitled to do so ... and no fat-lipped frog is going to tell me otherwise.

SEMICONFUSED PRINCE: I didn't mean to cause all this commotion. All I want is a wife, and I don't really care where she's lived or what she's eaten. In fact, I don't even care if she's covered with slime.

NARRATOR: Well, instead of trying to locate a bride in the mud and muck of the swamp, why don't you just go back to the castle and find a real live woman, instead of a former amphibian with big eyes and warts?

FROG #2: *(angrily)* Hey, hold on, mister. Just who do you think you are referring to my brothers as ugly?

NARRATOR: I didn't say they were ugly. Maybe strange and weird, but definitely not ugly.

SEMICONFUSED PRINCE: *(confused)* Hey, now I'm getting confused ... I mean, really confused! Wasn't this supposed to be a story about my search for the perfect wife? All I wanted was to find a green-eyed beauty here in the swamp whom I could take back to Mommy and Daddy. I really didn't mean to cause all this hassle.

WICKED WITCH: Hey, you know, he's right. In fact, I don't even need to be in this story. Right now, I should be over in another story trying to get that pesky Snow White to eat a couple of poisoned apples. So, if you'll excuse me, gentlemen.... *(she leaves)*

FROG #1: I've got to go, too. There's a bunch of big, fat, juicy dragonflies circling around that lily pad that are starting to make my tongue itch. *(he leaves)*

FROG #2: Yeah, that sounds good to me, too. *(he leaves)*

SEMICONFUSED PRINCE: Well, I guess that leaves just you and me, Narrator. And to be perfectly honest, I think I can end this story without your help.

NARRATOR: *(reluctantly)* Well, if you insist.... *(he or she leaves)*

SEMICONFUSED PRINCE: *(to audience)* And so, in the end, I went back and put an ad in the classified section of the castle newspaper. I got several phone calls and finally decided to marry an enchanted salamander with a great personality from the pond next door. But, of course, that's another story.

MR. TOAD
Just Another One of Those Crazy Amphibians

STAGING:

The narrator stands at a lectern. Each of the frog characters sits on a stool or chair in front of the audience. Mr. Toad stands up.

	Frog One	*Frog Two*	*Frog Three*
	X	X	X

Mr. Toad
X

Narrator
X

NARRATOR: *(often rambling)* Once upon a time, a long, long time ago, there was a giant swamp located near a big castle. In the swamp were all kinds of frogs, a few of whom just happened to be some enchanted princes who has been turned into frogs by a couple of passing witches who had nothing better to do with their time. As you might expect, there were some gorgeous ladies who happened to live in the nearby castle, all of whom were single and all of whom were looking for a nice handsome prince to marry so they could live happily ever after. Now it doesn't take a mental giant to figure out that those princesses would eventually find their way down to that smelly old swamp to kiss a few of the frogs to see if any one of them just happened to be an enchanted prince turned into a frog by one of those ever-present witches who just happen to show up in stories like these. So as you might expect, each day a group of the castle princesses would pack a picnic lunch and trip on down to the swamp to plant a few wet ones on the lips of any frogs they could catch. Well, it didn't take too long before the word got out that this swamp was the sight of a lot of kissing and smooching and hugging and other stuff. Soon, every frog and his brother wanted to get in on the action. It didn't make any difference that most of those guys weren't enchanted princes (just your usual everyday web-footed, bug-eyed, and green-slimed amphibians), but they sure knew a good thing when they heard it (you see, frogs aren't as dumb as you think). Well, the word began to reach other members of the animal kingdom, too. Most of the other animals were jealous of those lip-smackin' frogs, but because they had antlers, or feathers, or long bushy tails, they knew there was no way they could get in on the action. That is, except for one young enterprising animal—Mr. Toad.

MR. TOAD: *(to the audience)* Now, look. The way I figure it, I'm about as close to a frog as you can get. Sure, I'm a little uglier and a little bigger, but I think I'm a little bit smarter than those swamp-sucking frogs. So I'm going to hop right down to that old lily-covered pond and see if I can get me a couple of kisses and maybe even a hug or two from those lovely ladies in the castle.

NARRATOR: The next day Mr. Toad bought a ticket to Swampville and hopped on the next flight out of town. In no time, he was at the edge of the pond.

MR. TOAD: WOW! Look at that action. There must be more gorgeous ladies here than there are in the whole state of California. My dream come true!

FROG ONE: *(defiantly)* Hey, just a minute, buddy! Who do you think you are? If you think you're going to muscle in on our action, you've got another thing coming.

FROG TWO: *(angrily)* Yeah! Look, this here's our swamp. We came here when it was just a puddle on the map. Our hard work and long hours have turned it into the swamp it is today. So what if a couple of dumb maidens from the castle want to come down here every day and kiss all the brothers. That's just one of the benefits. But don't think that we're opening up the neighborhood to any green-skinned amphibian who just happens to hop on by.

MR. TOAD: Look, friends. I was just thinking ... as long as there's so much action here, you won't mind if one of your cousins stops by for a while to get a little smooching. It's not like I'm trying to take over your territory or something. I just thought you might want to spread the wealth around.

FROG THREE: *(guardedly)* Listen, it's not that we don't like you or anything, but as you can tell, we've really got a good thing going here. Every day there's a group of lovely ladies down here from the castle or a field trip of impressionable young maidens from the next county who want to find that special someone. So they come down here, kiss a few frogs, get some slime on their lips, and go home. Nobody gets hurt and everybody leaves with a big smile. But if we let in every Tom, Dick, and Harry, then there would be fewer hugs and fewer kisses for each of us. The maidens might eventually get wise to our scheme and figure that there couldn't be that many enchanted princes mucking around the kingdom. Pretty soon they'd stop coming down to the swamp and start some kind of dating service with bears or alligators or some of those other weird creatures.

FROG TWO: You can see that we've really got it made in the shade. If we lose this, then all we've got left in life is eating flies and sunning ourselves on some leftover lily pads.

MR. TOAD: *(pleading)* Hey, cousin. It's not like I'm trying to take over. I'm just looking for a little action ... just something to hold me over until the end of spring. Hey, look, the life of a toad is not the greatest. Sure, we're green and hop around a lot just like you; but, honestly, would you want to kiss a face like this? I just thought that if I could pass myself off as one of you guys I might get lucky. After all, to these maidens one amphibian probably looks like any other amphibian. So I get a couple of extra kisses — what's the harm?

FROG ONE: Well, he does have a point. I guess it wouldn't hurt if he hung around for a few days to pick up a few smooches and a hug or two. I mean, it's not like he's enchanted or anything. So, what do you say, guys?

FROG TWO: *(resignedly)* Well, I guess it's okay.

FROG THREE: *(reluctantly)* Yeah, I guess so. But I say that after one week old toad face here is history. Agreed?

**FROG ONE and
FROG TWO:** *(together)* Agreed!

MR. TOAD: Thanks, guys. Believe me, you've just made my day. Tell me, which of the lily pads gets the most action?

NARRATOR: And so it was that Mr. Toad was able to get lots of kisses and lots of hugs (and an occasional tummy tickle). When he returned home, he had quite a tale to tell all his brothers. And, as you might imagine, they were all green with envy.

DON'T KISS US, WE'RE JUST A BUNCH OF FROGS!

STAGING:

The narrator stands and may walk from frog to frog with a makeshift microphone. Each of the frogs is on a stool or sits on a chair.

```
                    Frog #1        Frog #2
                      X              X
              Frog #3        Frog #4
                X              X
      Narrator
        X
```

NARRATOR: We now take you down to "Frog Central" where this late-breaking story has just come in. It seems as though all the frogs in Swampville, U.S.A., have started a revolt and, boy, are they angry. I mean things are really hopping down there. Let's interview some of the amphibians involved. Excuse me, sir, would you mind if we talked with you?

FROG #1: Well, okay, but let's make it quick. I've got to get back to my lily pad for the midnight demonstration.

NARRATOR: Tell our viewers, sir, what all of this commotion is about.

FROG #1: Well, you see it's like this. We're just a bunch of lazy, fly-eating, green-skinned, slimy-lipped frogs trying to mind our own business. We don't hurt anyone, we keep to ourselves, and we stay out of trouble. But every time some beautiful princess is in town, she thinks we're all enchanted princes and she has to come down to the swamp to kiss as many of us as she can. YUCK!!!

FROG #2: *(forcefully)* Yeah, you tell 'em, Leroy.

FROG #1: So you see, we're getting just a little fed up with all of these beautiful princesses who have nothing better to do with their time than smooch a bunch of innocent frogs down here at the swamp.

NARRATOR: How often does this occur?

FROG #3:   *(indignantly)* Too often. All we want to do is paddle around the swamp, eat a bunch of flying insects, and live our happy, contented lives. But n-o-o-o-o-o-o-o-o-o-o, those silly little girls have to come down here every chance they get to play kissy-face with us. Frankly, it's becoming pretty disgusting.

NARRATOR: Well, how do the other frogs feel about it?

FROG #4:   *(excitedly)* We're all hopping mad! I mean, what gives those maidens the right to just come on down here any time they please to kiss every amphibian they see? Hey, just because one or two of us might be an enchanted prince or something doesn't give those beautiful maidens the right to kiss every single amphibian they see. We have rights, too, you know!

FROG #2:   Yeah, Harold's right. Any time we just want to sit out in the sun and catch a few rays, those stupid girls have to come down and see if they can turn one of us back into some Prince Charming or something. Boy, that ticks me off! Not only does it disturb our quiet lifestyle, but it interferes with my fly-eating routine. I haven't been able to eat more than two hundred flies in a single sitting since this kissing epidemic started.

FROG #1:   Yeah, and to make things even worse there's a new castle complex going up on the other end of the swamp. And you know what that means? More princesses will be moving into the neighborhood and, of course, more of them will want to come down to the swamp to plant their fat lips on each and every one of us. I mean that's really gross!!!

NARRATOR: It sounds as if you guys have a real problem on your hands. Have you thought about talking with the wicked witches to see if you can't work something out with them?

FROG #3:   We tried to, but they didn't pay any attention to our requests. They said it was their right to turn any prince in the kingdom into a frog and to place those frog princes in any swamp they wanted to. It was just our tough luck if all the maidens in the kingdom just happened to stop by our swamp to kiss every green amphibian they could find.

FROG #2: *(angrily)* And you know what really ticks me off? Not only do we have a bunch of enchanted frog princes hopping around here in green suits, but we've also got to teach them how to stick out their tongues so they can catch some flies every now and again so they won't starve. I mean, it's not like we have nothing better to do with our time. Believe me, I've had it up to here!

NARRATOR: It doesn't sound like there's an easy solution to this problem.

FROG #1: Yeah, and that's why we're on strike. We're refusing to eat any more flies or dragonflies. Let's just see what those princesses say when they're overrun by all kinds of insects and other creepy crawly things. They'll wish they had never messed around with us frogs. And maybe those witches will think twice about turning some stupid princes into frogs—which does nothing but upset the ecological balance in this place. And then maybe we'll get a little peace and quiet around here.

NARRATOR: So what would you say is your biggest complaint?

FROG #4: Trying to wipe all that red lipstick off our skin.

PICTURE THIS
It's a Photo Opportunity

STAGING:
The narrator stands to the side or in back of the two major characters. The two frogs stand in the front center of the staging area.

Narrator
X

          Felicia Frog   *Fanny Frog*
            X   **X**

NARRATOR: Once upon a time there were these frogs just sitting around the local swamp telling stories and such. Actually, I think it's only fair to tell you that these weren't just your everyday, ordinary frogs. No way, José. These were real live talking frogs—you know, the kind of frogs you find in all those other fairy tales. Except that these frogs were really bright, really smart, really intelligent. And, of course, they were all girls! In fact, this whole entire swamp was filled with nothing but girl frogs ... lots and lots of girl frogs. (For some reason, the writer decided not to have any boy frogs in this story.) So, let's listen in on a conversation two of these frogs were having one day.

FELICIA FROG: Say, did I hear that you were down around that stinky old castle the other day?

FANNY FROG: Yeah, that's right. I was just nosing around to see if anything interesting might be paddling around there. You know how long it's been since we've seen any good-lookin' guys around here. I just thought I might hop on down to the castle to look for some frog hunks or something.

FELICIA FROG: Why would you want to do a thing like that? I mean, we've got it made down here. All the flies we can eat, lots of lily pads to hop around on, and some of the smelliest and stinkiest swampland in the whole country. Why would you want to go and ruin all of that by bringing some dumb guys from the castle down here?

FANNY FROG: Yeah, I know. I just thought it might make things a little more interesting if we had a guy or two swim around the swamp every now and again. I mean, it's not like we're going to let them move in or anything.

FELICIA FROG: Well, maybe you're right. But you'd better be extra careful. You know, once you start associating with those frogmen types, the next thing you know they want to move in with you, start a family, and watch football games all weekend. I think you'd better take it nice and easy.

FANNY FROG: I already thought about that. What I'm going to do first is take my camera down to the castle, hide among the weeds, and photograph all the young dudes who pass by. Then when the pictures are developed I'm going to spread them out on my kitchen table, look them over real carefully, and decide which one or two I want to invite down here for a visit. Sounds like a great idea, don't you think?

FELICIA FROG: Yeah, I guess so. Just be careful!

NARRATOR: Several days pass.

FELICIA FROG: Hey, Fanny, why the long face? You burp up some flies or something?

FANNY FROG: No, it's not that at all. You remember that great plan I had with the camera and the castle down the road? Well, I went down there like I said, took more than five rolls of pictures, and dropped them off at the Drugs and Bugs store downtown. But I still haven't seen the pictures. I hope they didn't lose all those rolls of film.

FELICIA FROG: Don't worry about it. The same thing happened to me a few months ago. Eventually, they were found. As they say, someday your prints will come! Get it? Someday your prints will come! **HA HA HA HA** ha ha ha ha *ha ha ha ha ha ha ha ha....*

SO, WHO IS THIS KERMIT GUY, ANYWAY?

STAGING:
The four frogs can stand in a loose circle in the middle of the staging area. The narrator should sit on a tall stool off to the side.

Franz   *Fred*
Frog   *Frog*
X   X

Francis   *Frank*
Frog   *Frog*
X   X

Narrator
X

NARRATOR: It was just one of those days. You know, a day full of sunshine, a sky full of nice fat insects, lots of smells and odors coming up from the swamp, and tons and tons of mucky mud for everyone to hop around in. In other words, it was a perfect day in the swamp! It just so happened that a couple of the guys were sitting around the local fly bar discussing some of the latest happenings around the swamp and, of course, the results from that weekend's frog football game. It wasn't too long before the conversation got around to famous frogs — frogs who had made their mark in the world and had been immortalized in song, stories, and movies — but more about that later.

FRANZ FROG: *(thoughtfully)* Yeah, I remember those days. Those were the days when a frog was a frog. Those were the days when a frog wasn't afraid to shoot straight from the mouth ... wrap his tongue around every living insect he could find. Nowadays, these youngsters want their flies served on silver platters, or boiled, or fried, or even (gag) microwaved. What a bunch of wimps!!!

FRED FROG: You're absolutely right, Gramps. These kids don't know a good thing when they see it. They want stereos in the swamp and CDs on every lily pad so they can play their loud rock music day and night. Why can't kids today just act like we did when we were their age?

FRANCIS FROG: Now all they want to do is get through their tadpole stage as fast as they can and swim off to some big pond and make their mark in the world. They think they can be hotshot musicians or movie stars or TV producers. For most of them it's a dead-end road. They usually wind up on someone's dinner plate at some fancy-dancy French restaurant in the big city. If they'd only stay in their own neighborhood they wouldn't get into so much trouble.

FRANK FROG: *(disgusted)* Hmmmfp. Big shots!! Yeah, as soon as their skin turns green and their tongues get long enough to snag a few dragonflies they're off to the big time. Like that big famous frog ... what's 'is name? Kermit. Yeah, there's a real hotshot for ya. He gets lucky, makes a few appearances on TV, and the next thing you know he's buying some big castle in Hollywood, stocking the refrigerators with gourmet flies from Europe, and sipping on bottled swamp water from some faraway country we've never heard of before. I mean, who does this guy think he is, anyway?

FRED FROG: And did you hear he has his own chauffeur-driven lily pad with green racing stripes all over it? He takes it everywhere he goes and thinks he's the greatest thing since Prince Charming.

FRANCIS FROG: To be honest with you, I don't think he's got all that much talent. I mean, after all, how much talent does it take to sit on a log, sing a few songs, talk about the letters "H" and "R," and smile at the camera every once in a while. Heck, we could all do that with our eyes closed. What makes him so great?

FRANK FROG: Yeah, and get this. He gets to choose all his costars in his pictures. But do you think he'd call on his old friends from the local swamp? N-o-o-o-o-o-o-o. He now works with some smelly pig who wants to marry him, a bear who has cotton for a brain, and a bunch of wimps who look as though their noses got caught in an elevator door. I mean, let's get real, folks. Are these the kind of individuals you'd want to associate with down at your local fly store?

FRANZ FROG: Yeah, these kids. They just don't know what's good for them.

FRED FROG: *(dejectedly)* Honestly, I'm getting just a little sick and tired of all the publicity this Kermit guy is getting, while the rest of us working stiffs try to do an honest day's work down in the swamp and get nothin' in return. He's got about as much talent as the sales clerk down at Bugs 'R Us. In other words, ZIP!

FRANK FROG: *(angrily)* So who does he think he is? Does he ever come back to the old neighborhood? NO. Does he ever write and ask how we're doing? NO. Does he even care if we're getting enough flies in our diet? NO. Ever since he moved into the big time, he's not only forgotten where he's come from, but also all of his old friends. *(sarcastically)* Now his friends are a bunch of overstuffed cotton rags who sing about the people in their neighborhood and some stupid old letters in the alphabet. I mean, would you want to admit that your best friend was the letter "F"? Ha, Ha, Ha. What a joke. Hey guys, look at me. I'd like you to meet some of my friends. Here's the letter "Q," the letter "B," and my all-time best buddy, the letter "Z." Ha, ha, ha, ha, ha, ha. What a joke!!!

FRANCIS FROG: Hey, what do you say we change the subject. All this talk about that Kermit guy is making me hungry. Say, anybody ready for another round of grass-hoppers?

NARRATOR: And so it was that the conversation down at the local fly bar eventually turned to other things. And Kermit's name was never spoken again.

Part IV
SOME SHORT STORIES

(Actually, it's just the stories that are short ... these aren't really stories about short people as you might think because if they were, I would have to call them "Dwarf Stories" or "Gnome Stories" or "Leprechaun Stories" or "Troll Stories," and we already have plenty of those stories throughout this book, so these are just stories that are not as long as some of the other stories, although they could be just as long as those other ones, if I had had more time to make them longer; but you see, as I began to write them my cats got kinda sick and I had to take them to the vet and then there was this big snowstorm and the car broke down and I had to walk for miles and miles and miles and I didn't have my mittens on and I got sorta lost and then, by chance, I met this strange and enchanted frog [what else?] along the side of the road who promised to help me if I would help him find the really, really magic wand in the deep, dark dungeon of the evil and wicked stepmother's castle that would turn him back into the big handsome prince he really was ... s-o-o-o-o-o-o-o-o-o-o-o, anyway, are you now beginning to understand why these are short stories instead of those regular-length stories all the other fairy tale writers use in their books?... I hope so.)

(By the way, the cats are doing just fine. Thanks for asking.)

Well, if you have to know—these stories are really designed to serve as starters for your students' own self-created readers theatre stories. In other words, have students use one of these as the beginning or opening for a readers theatre story they may want to create. Students can add to them, modify them, or alter them in accordance with their own interests, logic, or warped senses of humor (neat idea, huh?).

THE TRIAL OF GOLDILOCKS
(You Can't Bear to Miss This One.
Get It? You Can't Bear....)

STAGING:

The narrator stands at a lectern or podium. The staging area is set up to look like a courtroom with the judge in the middle rear, a jury along one side, two tables (one for the prosecution, one for the defense), and a witness chair. Witnesses will move back and forth between the gallery and the witness chair.

```
                    Judge          (witness chair)
                      X                  X

Bailiff
   X
      Defense Attorney    Goldilocks              Prosecuting Attorney
            X                 X                          X
Snow White                                                              Narrator
   X                                                                       X
                              (gallery)
            X          X          X          X          X          X
      X          X          X          X          X          X
            X          X          X          X          X          X
```

NARRATOR: Once upon a time there was this maiden who walked around the deep and dark forest breaking into other characters' houses. It's not that she was trying to steal anything or hold up anybody, it's just that she was bored and didn't know what to do with herself. So she just walked into every little cottage, dwelling, house, or castle she could find. But, on this one day, she happened to pick the wrong house. Because, you see, this house belonged to the Three Bears, and not just any Three Bears, mind you. It so happened that these three bears were all upstanding citizens, and they weren't about to let any blonde-haired young maiden just climb into their house, eat all their porridge, sit in their chairs, and lie down on their beds without having her arrested and hauled off to jail. After all, these three bears certainly knew the law, and they didn't want all the other fairy tale characters to think that anybody could just come into a story, do anything he or she wanted, and live happily ever after. Oh, no!! Not these bears. So it was then that this Goldilocks character was arrested and jailed for breaking and entering. Several weeks later she was brought to trial in the courtroom of Judge Ima Wolf. We take you now to that trial.

BAILIFF:	*(officially)* The court will now come to order. The honorable Ima Bigbad Wolf presiding.
JUDGE:	Does the defense wish to make a statement?
DEFENSE ATTORNEY:	We do, your honor. My client has been accused of breaking and entering the Three Bears' house in the deep and dark forest. We will prove to this court that the Bears not only left their dwelling unlocked, but actually invited my client in to try their lousy porridge, sit in their lousy chairs, and lie down on their lousy beds. After all, your honor, the Three Bears own a furniture store and had been promoting their big Thanksgiving Day sale throughout the forest for several weeks. Certainly they expected other characters and creatures to come into their place of business to try out the furniture they were selling. And the porridge ... that was just a promotional giveaway for the store.
JUDGE:	Thank you. Does the prosecution wish to make a statement at this time?
PROSECUTING ATTORNEY:	Not at this time, Your Honor. Instead, we'd like to call our first witness to the stand. We'd like to call Snow White.
GOLDILOCKS:	*(in a loud whisper and sarcastically)* Yeah, like she'll know what she's talking about.
GALLERY:	*(mumble, mumble, mumble, talk, talk, talk)*
JUDGE:	*(loudly)* Court will come to order. Any more outbursts like that and I'll have the bailiff clear the courtroom.
PROSECUTING ATTORNEY:	Miss White, would you please tell the court your version of the story.
SNOW WHITE:	*(rambling)* Well, you see, it was like this. I was over in my cottage. Actually, it's not my cottage ... I just happen to live there with these seven funny little men who work down at the local diamond mine and who've asked me to keep their place clean for them while they're down in the mines singing "Hi, Ho, Hi, Ho, It's Off to Work We Go" and all kinds of other songs like that which I think helps them pass the time away while they're down deep in the caverns and caves of the mine searching for the....

JUDGE: *(frustrated)* Miss White, would you please just tell your story.

SNOW WHITE: Well, okay. Anyway, I was outside my cottage when I saw this Goldilocks character skipping through the forest. Now, I'm no Peeping Tom or anything like that, but I couldn't help noticing that she stopped at the Three Bears' cottage and looked in the window. It wasn't too long after that I saw her open the door and walk right in.

PROSECUTING ATTORNEY: And then what happened?

POSSIBLE CONCLUSIONS

1. The Three Little Pigs serve as character witnesses for Goldilocks.

2. Goldilocks is found guilty and is banished to another story.

3. Goldilocks is found innocent and has a big party. Unfortunately, Judge Ima Bigbad Wolf is inadvertently invited and winds up eating all the guests.

4. A frog hops on the witness stand, kisses Goldilocks, turns into a handsome prince, and rides off with Goldilocks into the sunset.

5. Your idea.

A STUPID STORY ABOUT A VERY SLOW TURTLE AND A VERY FAST RABBIT
(Except This Time the Ending's Different)

STAGING:

The narrator can be sitting on a tall stool. All of the animals can be standing in a circle or semicircle in the middle of the staging area.

Lizard
X

Deer X   X *Mouse*

Lion X   X *Iguana*

Kangaroo X   X *Turtle*

X   X

Earthworm   *Rabbit*

NARRATOR: Once upon a time, a long time ago, all the animals in the forest were in really great shape. In fact, they were in such good condition that they would always race each other just to see who was the fastest. Now you may think this was a pretty silly thing for animals to do, but just think about it. What else do animals do during the day except hang around and sleep and eat other animals? Not very much fun. So, one day, some of them got this really nifty idea to hold a bunch of races and see who was the fastest. The only problem was that the same animals always won the races. The rabbits always won on land and the eagles always won in the air and the sharks always won in the water. (Of course, all the other animals wanted to make sure that the sharks always won ... after all, just imagine how angry the sharks would have been had they lost. It would not have been a very pretty sight.) So, it wasn't too long before some of the other animals (who weren't very bright to begin with) finally caught on that they were getting their pants run off by a bunch of hotshot rabbits, dive-bomber birds, and bad-tempered sharks. So one day all the land animals decided to have a meeting to see what could be done.

DEER: Look, I don't know about you guys, but I've had it up to here watching the rear ends of those hotshot rabbits in every race we have against them. I mean, who do they think they are, showing off and beating us every chance they get?

LIZARD: I'm with Deer. Frankly, I'm getting sick and tired of having those overgrown rodents beat us silly every chance they get.

MOUSE: *(defiantly)* Now, just a minute. Watch who you're calling a rodent. Just because I live with a bunch of rats doesn't mean you have a right to call me names.

LION: *(soothingly)* Okay, okay. Let's just hold on here a minute, fellas. It's obvious that none of us is ever going to beat those guys in any kind of race. So what we need to do is trick them.

EARTHWORM: What are you suggesting? We've all raced those pesky rabbits, and we've all lost. There's nobody left who hasn't raced and lost against those guys.

LION: Well, I've got this plan. See, usually rabbits think they are so-o-o-o-o-o-o cool and that there is no one around who can beat them. What we've done in the past is put our fastest guys up against them. So what I'm suggesting is that we put our slowest guy up against their fastest guy. In other words, we use Turtle as our racer in the next race.

IGUANA: *(confused)* I don't get it. Turtle is about as slow as a crate of molasses in January. My granny could beat him with all her legs tied behind her back.

LION: That's just the point. We'll make them think they're going to win the race without even trying. They'll think they're racing Turtle, but they really won't be.

KANGAROO: I think I'm a little confused.

LION: Just listen, here's what we're going to do.

POSSIBLE CONCLUSIONS

1. Turtle decides that he doesn't want anything to do with the race and backs out.

2. Rabbit gets a bad case of athlete's foot and has to withdraw from the race. Turtle wins by default.

3. During the race, Rabbit gets eaten by the Big Bad Wolf and Turtle gets run over by a semi truck.

4. During the race, Rabbit is approached by an agent for Nike shoes and signs a multimillion dollar contract.

5. All of the animals ambush Rabbit and Turtle in the middle of the race and cook up a big batch of rabbit stew and turtle soup.

6. Your idea.

THE INCIDENT WITH THE PUMPKIN EATER FAMILY (And Why Would Anyone Want to Live Inside a Pumpkin Anyway?)

STAGING:

The narrator can be seated on a chair to one side of the staging area. The other characters can be standing or seated on stools.

Tom Tomato   *Carl Carrot*
   X   X

Carla Corn   *Betty Bean*
   X   X

Rose Radish
X

Narrator
X

NARRATOR: Once upon a time there was this guy named Peter, and let's just say that he wasn't too bright. He was far too lazy to build a house for his family so he just moved the wife and kids into a used pumpkin on the other side of town. Actually, it wasn't such a bad idea ... they never starved 'cause all they had to do was eat the walls and nibble on the seeds they found scattered throughout the house. In fact, all the townspeople started calling him Peter Peter Pumpkin Eater, which was sorta an unusual name, but it fit.

Things were all right for a while until the pumpkin started going bad ... that is, it started to become really rotten. Smells would come from the pumpkin and flies would circle the top. The townspeople began complaining about the stench and would often stop to talk to each other about it at the local shopping mall.

TOM TOMATO: *(angrily)* Can you believe that guy? First he puts his whole family inside an old jack-o'-lantern and then lets it get so rotten that no one can go anywhere near it.

CARL CARROT: *(disgustedly)* Yeah, and to tell you the truth I'm getting pretty sick of it. I can't even go outside and sit on my back porch anymore—the stench is so bad.

CARLA CORN: Whew! Stinky! It's so bad that my ears are starting to curl and kernels are beginning to fall off my entire body.

BETTY BEAN: It's really becoming disgusting. After all that pumpkin's done for him and he just lets it rot.

ROSE RADISH: Something's got to be done.

POSSIBLE CONCLUSIONS

1. The town vegetables decide to get together in a large pot and discuss their situation.

2. A bunch of high school kids come along, pick up the pumpkin, and throw it against the side of a house.

3. Mrs. Pumpkin Eater decides to separate from Peter and takes the kids and moves to a vegetable garden in Oklahoma.

4. Peter is arrested for eating his own house.

5. Your idea.

CHICKEN LITTLE AND THE FOOD FIGHT IN THE SCHOOL CAFETERIA

STAGING:

The narrator can sit on a tall stool off to the side of the staging area. The other characters sit on chairs as they might in a school cafeteria.

		Turkey Lurkey	Goosey Loosey
		X	X
Chicken Little			
X			
		Ducky Lucky	Swany Dawny
		X	X
Narrator			
X			

CHICKEN LITTLE: *(very excited)* The sky is falling! The sky is falling!

NARRATOR: Now, wait just a minute here.

CHICKEN LITTLE: *(very excited)* The sky is falling! The sky is falling!

NARRATOR: *(impatiently)* Now, just hold on, will ya. I'm trying to set up this story, and all you're doing is running around like some birdbrain. Just pipe down for a second!

CHICKEN LITTLE: *(very softly)* The sky is falling.

NARRATOR: Okay. So now everyone knows that the sky is falling. But just give me a few moments to give the audience some background information so that they'll be able to enjoy this story. Okay?

See, once upon a time there was this student in school who was not what we would call bright. In fact, he probably had so many screws loose in his head that he sounded like someone's toolbox. Anyway, let's just say that he was not too swift in the intelligence department.

109

So one day this guy was sitting in the school cafeteria when someone accidentally (I mean really accidentally) threw some Jello across five rows of tables and hit this "Little" guy in the back of the head. This "Little" guy looked all around to see where the big slug of green Jello had come from, but he didn't see a thing so he went back to eating the seeds and berries on his tray.

TURKEY LURKEY: Hey, look guys. This Chicken Little guy obviously has left his brains out in the sun too long. What do you say we get something started?

GOOSEY LOOSEY: What do you suggest?

TURKEY LURKEY: Maybe we can get him to think that the sky is falling down. He's just stupid enough to go running around the school yelling something dumb like, "The sky is falling, the sky is falling!"

DUCKY LUCKY: Great idea, Turk. But how are you going to get him to believe that?

TURKEY LURKEY: I say we get a food fight started behind his back. Start throwing stuff like the mystery meat patties and the cornbread and the green peas and a couple of cartons of milk. He's just dumb enough to believe that all of that stuff would be falling out of the sky. Then we can yell that the sky is, indeed, falling down on us.

SWANY DAWNY: Wow, what a neat idea! I can't wait to see what he does when he feels a glob of chocolate pudding hit him in the face.

TURKEY LURKEY: Okay, now here's the plan....

POSSIBLE CONCLUSIONS

1. The animals start the food fight, but just as they do, the principal, Pheasant Pleasant, walks in and gets hit by a plate of spaghetti.

2. Chicken Little hides under the table and reads the *Old Farmer's Almanac*.

3. The noise disturbs Foxy Loxy, and he comes over and eats everyone for his lunch.

4. Chicken Little gets really mad and pushes a big plate of canned corn in Turkey Lurkey's face and tells him, "Eat this, birdbrain!"

5. Your idea.

JUST A BUNCH OF FROGS STANDING AROUND AND TALKING

STAGING:

The narrator stands to one side of the staging area. The characters can all sit on tall stools or chairs.

A-Frog   *B-Frog*

X   X

C-Frog   *D-Frog*

X   X

Narrator

X

NARRATOR: It wasn't a very good day in the neighborhood swamp. In fact, all the frogs were excited, and angry, about the latest news that had just come down from the nearby castle. Indeed, they were so upset that they didn't see the swarm of fat flies that passed by overhead. So, let's look in and see what we can discover.

A-FROG: *(disgusted)* Can you believe it? It's incredible. Why would they ever want to do something like that?

B-FROG: *(angrily)* Here we are, minding our own business and these hotshots from the big city just think they can waltz in here, drain our swamp, and build some high-rise condos for those rich weasels and foxes. I mean, I'm really irritated.

C-FROG: This has got to be the lowest of the low. We mind our business, eat only the flies in our own neighborhood, keep our lily pads neat and clean, and this is the thanks we get. Is there anything we can do about it?

D-FROG: I'm not sure there is. You know how those big city lawyers are. A couple of contracts, a few signatures, and they now own some of the richest real estate in the whole kingdom.

111

B-FROG: You know what I think? I think it was those toads down at the south end of the pond who sold us out. You know how they're always trying to move into our territory. Remember that incident with the dragonflies a couple of years ago? Well, they never forgot that, and now I think they're trying to get even.

C-FROG: Well, well, well. Isn't that a hoot! Just because they're green and have warts all over their skin they think that they can turn over some prime real estate to those big city yahoos and retire fat and rich on some Florida swampland for the rest of their lives. I think we've been had, guys.

A-FROG: Boy, we're really in a mess now. In about sixty days those bulldozers will plow through here tearing up all our pads and draining all our yards and then we're outta here ... lock, stock, and barrel.

D-FROG: Wait a minute! I think I've got a plan that just might work. A plan that just might let us keep our lily pads and our flies and our swamp and really teach those toads a lesson.

B-FROG: What do you have in mind?

POSSIBLE CONCLUSIONS

1. The frogs disguise themselves as toads and secretly drain the toads' swamp and build their own condos.

2. The frogs organize all of the dragonflies to dive-bomb the toads and scare them away from the swamp.

3. A wicked witch turns all the frogs into handsome princes who all move to the castle and marry incredibly beautiful princesses. The toads are left all by themselves in the swamp.

4. A fire-breathing dragon roasts all the toads for dinner.

5. Your idea.

Part V
APPENDIXES

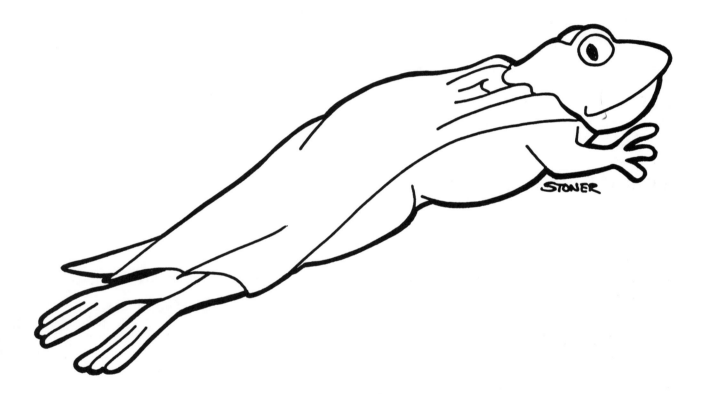

APPENDIX A: A BIBLIOGRAPHY OF
SOME FAIRY TALES, INTERESTING BOOKS, AND
OTHER GREAT STORIES
(From "Once Upon a Time" Time)
THAT CAN BE SHARED WITH YOUR STUDENTS
EVERY ONCE IN A WHILE

Aesop. *Aesop's Fables*. New York: Viking, 1981.

Andersen, Hans Christian. *Thumbelina*. New York: Dial, 1979.

_____. *The Ugly Duckling*. New York: Harcourt Brace Jovanovich, 1979.

Asbjørnsen, Peter Christian, and Jørgen E. Moe. *Three Billy Goats Gruff*. New York: Clarion, 1981.

Brett, Jan. *Beauty and the Beast*. New York: Clarion, 1989.

_____. *Goldilocks and the Three Bears*. New York: Dodd, Mead, 1987.

Cauley, Lorinda Bryan. *Goldilocks and the Three Bears*. New York: Putnam, 1981.

_____. *The Town Mouse and the Country Mouse*. New York: Putnam, 1984.

De Beaumont, Madame Le Prince. *Beauty and the Beast*. New York: Crown, 1986.

dePaola, Tomie. *The Comic Adventures of Old Mother Hubbard and Her Dog*. San Diego, Calif.: Harcourt Brace Jovanovich, 1981.

_____. *Tomie dePaola's Favorite Nursery Tales*. New York: Putnam, 1986.

_____. *Tomie dePaola's Mother Goose*. New York: Putnam, 1985.

de Regniers, Beatrice Schenk. *Red Riding Hood: Retold in Verse*. New York: Atheneum, 1977.

Domanska, Janina. *Little Red Hen*. New York: Macmillan, 1973.

Emberley, Barbara. *The Story of Paul Bunyan*. Englewood Cliffs, N.J.: Prentice-Hall, 1963.

Galdone, Paul. *Cinderella*. New York: McGraw-Hill, 1978.

_____. *The Gingerbread Boy*. New York: Clarion, 1983.

_____. *The Hare and the Tortoise*. New York: McGraw-Hill, 1962.

_____. *Henny Penny*. New York: Clarion, 1984.

_____. *Jack and the Beanstalk*. New York: Clarion, 1982.

_____. *Little Bo-Peep*. New York: Clarion, 1982.

_____. *The Little Red Hen*. New York: McGraw-Hill, 1985.

_____. *Little Red Riding Hood*. New York: McGraw-Hill, 1974.

_____. *The Magic Porridge Pot*. New York: Clarion, 1976.

_____. *Old Mother Hubbard and Her Dog*. New York: McGraw-Hill, 1960.

_____. *Rumplestiltskin*. New York: Clarion, 1985.

_____. *Three Aesop Fox Fables*. New York: Clarion, 1971.

_____. *The Three Bears*. New York: Clarion, 1985.

_____. *Three Little Kittens*. New York: Clarion, 1986.

_____. *The Three Little Pigs*. New York: Clarion, 1984.

Grimm, Jakob, and Wilhelm Grimm. *The Bremen Town Musicians*. New York: Harper & Row, 1987.

_____. *Cinderella*. New York: Greenwillow, 1981.

_____. *The Donkey Prince*. New York: Doubleday, 1977.

_____. *The Elves and the Shoemaker*. Chicago: Follett, 1967.

_____. *Favorite Tales from Grimm*. New York: Four Winds Press, 1982.

_____. *The Frog Prince*. New York: Scholastic, 1987.

_____. *Grimm's Fairy Tales: Twenty Stories Illustrated by Arthur Rackham*. New York: Viking, 1973.

_____. *Hansel and Gretel*. New York: Morrow, 1980.

_____. *Little Red Riding Hood*. New York: Atheneum, 1988.

_____. *Popular Folk Tales: The Brothers Grimm*. New York: Doubleday, 1978.

_____. *Rapunzel*. New York: Holiday House, 1987.

_____. *Rumplestiltskin*. New York: Four Winds Press, 1973.

_____. *The Shoemaker and the Elves*. New York: Lothrop, Lee & Shepard, 1983.

_____. *The Sleeping Beauty*. New York: Atheneum, 1979.

_____. *Snow White*. Boston: Little, Brown, 1974.

_____. *Snow White and Rose Red*. New York: Delacorte, 1965.

_____. *Snow White and the Seven Dwarfs*. New York: Farrar, Straus, & Giroux, 1987.

_____. *Tom Thumb*. New York: Walck, 1974.

Haley, Gail. *Jack and the Bean Tree*. New York: Crown, 1986.

Harper, Wilhelmina. *The Gunniwolf*. New York: Dutton, 1967.

Hutchinson, Veronica S. *Henny Penny*. Boston: Little, Brown, 1976.

Ivimey, John W. *Complete Version of Ye Three Blind Mice*. New York: Warne, 1979.

Jacobs, Joseph. *Jack and the Beanstalk*. New York: Putnam, 1983.

_____. *The Three Little Pigs*. New York: Atheneum, 1980.

Kellogg, Steven. *Chicken Little*. New York: Morrow, 1985.

_____. *Paul Bunyan*. New York: Morrow, 1974.

_____. *Pecos Bill*. New York: Morrow, 1986.

Lobel, Arnold. *The Random House Book of Mother Goose*. New York: Random House, 1986.

Marshall, James. *Goldilocks and the Three Bears*. New York: Dial, 1988.

_____. *Red Riding Hood*. New York: Dial, 1987.

Ormerod, Jan. *The Story of Chicken Licken*. New York: Lothrop, Lee & Shepard, 1986.

Perrault, Charles. *Cinderella*. New York: Dial, 1985.

_____. *Little Red Riding Hood*. New York: Scholastic, 1971.

_____. *Puss in Boots*. New York: Clarion, 1976.

_____. *The Sleeping Beauty*. New York: Viking, 1972.

Provensen, Alice, and Martin Provensen. *Old Mother Hubbard*. New York: Random House, 1982.

Southey, Robert. *The Three Bears*. New York: Putnam, 1984.

Stevens, Janet. *Goldilocks and the Three Bears*. New York: Holiday House, 1986.

Still, James. *Jack and the Wonder Beans*. New York: Putnam, 1977.

Watts, Bernadette. *Goldilocks and the Three Bears*. New York: Holt, Rinehart & Winston, 1985.

Wildsmith, Brian. *Brian Wildsmith's Mother Goose*. New York: Oxford University Press, 1982.

APPENDIX B: A SWAMPFUL OF STRANGE, WEIRD, AND FUNKY TITLES KIDS CAN USE TO WRITE THEIR OWN READERS THEATRE SCRIPTS

Okay, I know what you're saying. This guy has really gone out on the end of a limb (although there will be many of you who will rightfully argue that I fell off the limb many pages ago ... but let's not get personal). So, anyway, what I've done is to cogitate (now there's a five-dollar word for you) some potential and possible titles your students might like to experiment with in terms of developing and designing their own readers theatre scripts (of course, your students are not permitted to use any other titles except these ... just kidding, just kidding).

I have often found it advantageous to divide my class into small groups and encourage each team to first brainstorm for as many stories, legends, and tales they can remember. All of these are recorded on the chalkboard. Then, groups are encouraged to develop weird and wacky tales for selected stories. These are also shared with the whole class. Later, each group will select its favorite title and begin creating a readers theatre script. This approach supports a process orientation to writing and stimulates an atmosphere of creative thinking.

Although you are certainly encouraged to use some of these suggested titles, it will be valuable for your students to have opportunities to generate their own titles. No doubt they will come up with some equally weird and strange titles for their stories (as well as some equally weird and strange stories). What you will discover is students who are not only immersed in the creativity of readers theatre, but also a whole classroom of students who will want to use all their language arts skills (reading, writing, speaking, listening) in meaningful and productive contexts.

1. Rip Van Winkle Snores and Makes the Whole Town Very Angry for About Twenty Years

2. Paul Bunyan Was a Wimp (Sort Of)

3. The Ugly Duckling Sues His Parents for Bad Genes

4. Old MacDonald Had a Farm That Was Bought by a Developer Who Wanted to Turn It into a Condominium

5. Mary Had a Little Lamb That Made a Big Mistake on the Classroom Floor

6. The Three Blind Mice Get a Seeing Eye Dog and Then Something Really Terrible Happens

7. Old Mother Hubbard Went to the Cupboard and Then Got Very Very Sick at What She Saw

8. Mother Goose Is Really a Duck with a Complexion Problem

9. London Bridge Is Falling Down ("Help, I've Fallen and I Can't Get Up!")

10. The Farmer in the Dell, the Farmer in the Dell, Hi Ho the Derry Oh, the Farmer in the Dell (and What the Heck Is a Dell, Anyway?)

11. The Three Bears Wander into Yellowstone Park and Begin to Steal Picnic Baskets

12. Snow White Finally Gets a New Name

13. Red Riding Hood Finally Gets a New Name

14. Sleeping Beauty Finally Gets a New Name

15. Everyone with a Stupid Name Finally Gets a New Name

16. The Evil Stepmother Turns into the Real Nice Stepmother Who Bakes Gingerbread Cookies for All the Kids

17. Cinderella Decides That She Doesn't Want to Dance with the Prince After All and Changes the End of Her Story

18. The Hare and the Tortoise Have a Race, but They Both Fall Asleep and Never Finish It

19. The Three Billy Goats Gruff Meet the Three Bears and the Three Little Pigs and They All Have a Wild and Crazy Party

20. Hansel and Gretel Move to Another Forest and Never Meet the Evil Witch

21. Jack Invites the Giant and His Wife over to the House for Roast Beef, Mashed Potatoes, and Corn on the Cob

22. The Absent-Minded Wizard Turns the Prince into a Smelly Old Skunk Instead of a Frog

23. The Three Little Pigs Hire a New Architect

24. Beauty and the Beast Turn Their Story into a Major Motion Picture and Make Tons of Money

25. The Fairy Godmother Loses Her Wand and Really Messes up Everything

26. "Cinderella — Get a Life!"

27. The Fire-Breathing Dragon Finally Uses Mouthwash (and, Boy, What a Difference!)

28. The Seven Dwarfs Form a Union and Strike for More Lines in the Story

29. The Princess Really Goes Crazy and Demands Plates and Plates of Frog Legs for Dinner

30. Chicken Little and the Incident at the Fast Food Restaurant

31. Little Boy Blue and Little Red Riding Hood Get Together to Create Little Kid Purple

32. The Gingerbread Man Gets Baked at 350° for Fifteen to Twenty Minutes

33. Little Jack Horner Sat in His Corner and Nobody Paid Any Attention to Him

APPENDIX C: RESOURCES
(The Stuff You Always Find at the
End of a Book)

MAGAZINE ARTICLES
ABOUT READERS THEATRE

Busching, B. A. "Readers Theatre: An Education for Language and Life." *Language Arts* 58 (1981): 330-38.

Henning, K. "Drama Reading: An Ongoing Classroom Activity at the Elementary School Level." *Elementary English* 51 (1974): 48-51.

Post, R. M. "Readers Theatre as a Method of Teaching Literature." *English Journal* 64 (1974): 69-72.

Wertheimer, A. "Story Dramatization in the Reading Center." *English Journal* 64 (1974): 85-87.

BOOKS ABOUT READERS THEATRE

Coger, L. I., and M. R. White. *Readers Theatre Handbook: A Dramatic Approach to Literature*. Glenview, Ill.: Scott, Foresman, 1982.

Johnson, T. D., and D. R. Louis. *Bringing It All Together: A Program for Literacy*. Portsmouth, N.H.: Heinemann, 1990.

Maclay, J. H. *Readers Theatre: Toward a Grammar of Practice*. New York: Random House, 1971.

Sloyer, S. *Readers Theatre: Story Dramatization in the Classroom*. Urbana, Ill.: National Council for Teachers of English, 1982.

Tanner, F. *Creative Communication: Projects in Acting, Speaking, Oral Reading*. Pocatello, Idaho: Clark Publishing, 1979.

SOURCES FOR ADDITIONAL
READERS THEATRE SCRIPTS
(Not That You'd Ever Want to Get Any More Scripts
Other Than the Really Clever Ones Presented in This Book)

Barchers, S. *Readers Theatre for Beginning Readers*. Englewood, Colo.: Teacher Ideas Press, 1993.

D.O.K., P.O. Box 605, East Aurora, N.Y. 14052.

Economy, 1901 N. Walnut, Oklahoma City, Okla. 73125.

Georges, C., and C. Cornett. *Reader's Theatre*. Buffalo, N.Y.: D.O.K., 1990.

Institute for Readers' Theatre, P.O. Box 17193, San Diego, Calif. 92117.

Latrobe, K. H., C. Casey, and L. A. Gann. *Social Studies Readers Theatre for Young Adults*. Englewood, Colo.: Teacher Ideas Press, 1991.

Latrobe, K. H., and M. K. Laughlin. *Readers Theatre for Young Adults*. Englewood, Colo: Teacher Ideas Press, 1989.

Laughlin, M. K., P. T. Black, and K. H. Latrobe. *Social Studies Readers Theatre for Children*. Englewood, Colo.: Teacher Ideas Press, 1991.

Laughlin, M. K., and K. H. Latrobe. *Readers Theatre for Children*. Englewood, Colo.: Teacher Ideas Press, 1990.

Reader's Theatre Script Service, P.O. Box 178333, San Diego, Calif. 92177; (619) 961-8778.

About the Author

Anthony D. Fredericks

Tony is definitely not an enchanted prince! He most certainly does not eat flies (although he does have a particular fondness for homemade macadamia nut cookies [hint, hint, hint]). And he currently does not live in a swamp. But he does love frogs (on occasion, he's even had a frog or two in his throat)! And, he has been known to spend a lot of time in muck, squishy, and oozy places (but, then, that's another story altogether).

Tony is a former classroom teacher and reading specialist. He is a frequent presenter and storyteller at conferences, reading councils, schools, and in-service meetings throughout North America. In addition to this book, he has written more than 30 other teacher resource books in the areas of science, social studies, and language arts. Additionally, he is a celebrated children's author, having written an impressive array of nonfiction books for kids, including the award winning *Weird Walkers* and *Clever Camouflagers*, both of which include stories about some really strange four-legged amphibians.

Tony is currently a professor (yes, he's now one of those) at York College in York, Pennsylvania, where he teaches methods courses in reading, language arts, science, and social studies. He describes himself as a nine-year-old boy trapped inside a middle-aged body." Despite rumors to the contrary, he does not have slimy skin, webbed feet, or warts. He is, however, married to a beautiful enchanted princess!

from Teacher Ideas Press

HOLIDAY READERS THEATRE
Charla R. Pfeffinger

Celebrate historical and cultural events, from the seven days of Kwanzaa to the secrets of Mardi Gras, with this wonderful collection of more than 25 reproducible scripts. **Grades 3–8.**
ix, 181p. 8½x11 paper ISBN 1-56308-162-8

¡TEATRO! Hispanic Plays for Young People
Angel Vigil

Actors and audience members experience and learn more about Hispanic culture and traditions of the American Southwest with these 14 reproducible scripts. **Grades 3–9.**
xviii, 169p. 8½x11 paper ISBN 1-56308-371-X

SOCIAL STUDIES READERS THEATRE FOR CHILDREN: Scripts and Script Development
Mildred Knight Laughlin, Peggy Tubbs Black, and Margery Kirby Loberg

These 14 reproducible tall tale scripts and 60 suggested scripts for student writing are based on passages from selected books about colonial America and the Revolutionary War. **Grades 4–6.**
xi,189p. 8½x11 paper ISBN 0-87287-865-1

READERS THEATRE FOR CHILDREN: Scripts and Script Development
Mildred knight Laughlin and Kathy Howard Latrobe

Using readers theatre is a snap with this delightful work. It shows you how to use readers theatre, gives you reproducible scripts, and has suggested script outlines that children may use to develop their own scripts. **Grades 4–6.**
xi,131p. 8½x11 paper ISBN 0-87287-753-1

AMAZING AMERICAN WOMEN: Forty Fascinating 5-Minute Reads
Kendall Haven

These concise, action-packed stories of some of the women who have helped shape our nation will enlighten and inspire all. **All Levels.**
xxii, 305p. paper ISBN 1-56308-291-8

JOURNAL KEEPING WITH YOUNG PEOPLE
Barbara Steiner and Kathleen C. Phillips

In this guide you'll find myriad possibilities for using journals with young people. It includes project ideas, techniques, guidelines, tips, and lists of additional resources. **Grades 4–9.**
xiii, 183p. paper ISBN 0-87287-872-4

HINTS FOR TEACHING SUCCESS IN MIDDLE SCHOOL
Robert E. Rubinstein

This enlightening overview of the teaching profession pinpoints what is really needed in the teacher/student relationship and provides classroom-tested strategies and suggestions that REALLY work.
xiv,160p. paper ISBN 1-56308-124-5

RIP-ROARING READS FOR RELUCTANT TEEN READERS
Gale W. Sherman and Bette D. Ammon

Contemporary, spellbinding titles (20 for grades 5–8 and 20 for grades 9–12) reflect a variety of genres and themes that kids really enjoy. **Grades 5–12.**
ix, 164p. 8½x11 paper ISBN 1-56308-094-X

For a free catalog or to order these or any other TIP titles, please contact:
   Teacher Ideas Press • Dept. B17 • P.O. Box 6633 • Englewood, CO 80155
   Phone: 1-800-237-6124, ext. 1 • Fax: 1-303-220-8843 • E-mail: lu-books@lu.com

⌐